CULTURE SMART!
MAURITIUS

Tim Cleary

·K·U·P·E·R·A·R·D·

ISBN 978 1 85733 542 2
This book is also available as an e-book: eISBN 978 1 85733 546 0

British Library Cataloguing in Publication Data
A CIP catalogue entry for this book is available from the
British Library

Copyright © 2011 Kuperard

First published in Great Britain 2011
by Kuperard, an imprint of Bravo Ltd
59 Hutton Grove, London N12 8DS
Tel: +44 (0) 20 8446 2440 Fax: +44 (0) 20 8446 2441
www.culturesmart.co.uk
Inquiries: sales@kuperard.co.uk

Distributed in the United States and Canada
by Random House Distribution Services
1745 Broadway, New York, NY 10019
Tel: +1 (212) 572-2844 Fax: +1 (212) 572-4961
Inquiries: csorders@randomhouse.com

Series Editor Geoffrey Chesler
Design Bobby Birchall

Printed in Malaysia

Cover image: *Architectural detail of a Hindu temple, Mauritius* ©iStockphoto.com
The photographs on pages 20, 60, 66, 93, 97, 101, 108, and 132 are reproduced
by permission of the author.
Images on the following pages reproduced under Creative Commons
Attribution-Share Alike 3.0 Unported license: 13 © Shardan; 14, 44, 118
(above), and 127 © Simisa; 16, 62, and 63 © B.navez; 51 and 65 © Sblaval at fr.
Wikipedia; 97 © Pancrat; 118 (below) © HallvardLid; 124 (no name given);
131 (above) © Virtualage; and 138 © Thierry
Images on these pages reproduced under Creative Commons Attribution-
Share Alike 2.0 Generic license: 37 © Tim Parkinson and 91 © Avinash
Meetoo. On page 110, Creative Commons Attribution-Share Alike 2.0
Germany © LonelyPlanet on the German Wikipedia; and on page 104,
Creative Commons Attribution-No Derivatives 2.0 Generic © bengal*foam
On pages 74 © Dhondusaxena; 89 © Tejal Patel; and 131 (below) © Jean Andy

About the A

TIM CLEARY has a BA in French from the University of Leeds, where he specialized in Creole languages and the Francophone world, and an MA in Linguistics from the School of Oriental and African Studies, University of London. He has worked as a translator (French to English), has lived in Mauritius, and in 2010 married a Mauritian, with whom he is learning to speak Kreol. Tim currently lives in London and works at the famous Stanfords map and travel bookshop in Covent Garden, but he visits Mauritius regularly. He enjoys listening to Mauritian sega music and drinking the occasional can of Phoenix lager.

**The Culture Smart! series is continuing to expand.
For further information and latest titles visit
www.culturesmart.co.uk**

The publishers would like to thank **CultureSmart!**Consulting for its help in researching and developing the concept for this series.

CultureSmart!Consulting creates tailor-made seminars and consultancy programs to meet a wide range of corporate, public-sector, and individual needs. Whether delivering courses on multicultural team building in the USA, preparing Chinese engineers for a posting in Europe, training call-center staff in India, or raising the awareness of police forces to the needs of diverse ethnic communities, it provides essential, practical, and powerful skills worldwide to an increasingly international workforce.

For details, visit www.culturesmartconsulting.com

CultureSmart!Consulting and **CultureSmart!** guides have both contributed to and featured regularly in the weekly travel program "Fast Track" on BBC World TV.

contents

contents

NOTE ON SPELLING

Throughout the text, you will find many Kreol words and others derived from Asian, African, and Malagasy languages. Many of these words are often only spoken, and others have variable spellings. In the case of Kreol words, we try to follow the spelling adopted in the *Diksioner Morisien* (the first monolingual Kreol dictionary) by Arnaud Carpooran.

When referring to the creole language spoken in Mauritius, we have used the spelling "Kreol" to distinguish it from "Creole," a term used to refer to Mauritians of predominantly African and Malagasy ancestry.

Map of Mauritius

introduction

A small, exotic, multicultural island nation in the middle of the Indian Ocean, Mauritius gives the impression of a paradise on earth. Graceful palm trees, fine sandy beaches, blissful lagoons, and endless fields of lush, green sugarcane help to reinforce its romantic image.

This island nation is a very new society, forged over the past three centuries. Although similar in many ways to neighboring Réunion and the Seychelles, and to Caribbean cultures such as Trinidad and Tobago where there is also a mixed population of African and Indian ancestry, Mauritius actually has a much greater South and East Asian influence than these islands. But that is not the whole story: a strong French cultural and linguistic heritage persists, even though the island was taken over and ruled by Britain for a hundred and fifty-eight years, and you only have to scratch the surface of many a Mauritian custom to find its African and Malagasy roots.

Although it would be difficult to claim a single overarching identity for the Mauritian people, certain traits recur in the accounts of foreign visitors: hospitality, warmth, and friendliness, albeit with an unexpected element of reserve. Above all, the most defining characteristic of the Mauritians is their multiculturalism. The island's rich cultural diversity reflects the origins of the people who settled there, and Mauritian language, food, and religion form an intoxicating medley.

Other customs have been created locally and have become part of an authentic native culture that is shared by all—such as sega, the distinctive, lively, and popular music of Mauritius.

Mauritius is not always, however, the haven of peace, love, and understanding that it may at first sight seem, and the reality is more complex and nuanced. Although today many Western and European-style customs are encroaching on both private and public life, Mauritians are ambivalent about this, and ancestral traditions are still firmly established in the daily lives of the population. On the downside, the Mauritians have a tendency to fight among themselves and to create communal stereotypes of their compatriots—Creoles are characterized as lazy and fun-loving, Indo- and Sino-Mauritians as clannish and nepotistic, and Franco-Mauritians as insular and racist, for example. However, the march of modernization and globalization means that many young, socially mobile Mauritians now share a common culture and outlook on life, where the sense of being Mauritian far outweighs ancestral ties and divisive communalism.

This book aims to make sense of the modern and the traditional, of the complex legacy of shared and ancestral cultures. It will help you to navigate your way through the contradictions of Mauritian society and to enrich your experience of this fascinating and beautiful island.

Key Facts

Official Name	République de Maurice (Republic of Mauritius)	
Capital City	Port Louis (pop. 150,000)	
Main Towns	Beau Bassin, Rose Hill, Quatre Bornes, Vacoas, Phoénix, Curepipe, Mahébourg, Port Mathurin (Rodrigues)	
Area	788 sq. miles (2,040 sq. km), incl. dependencies of Rodrigues, Saint Brandon, and Agalega	
Climate	Tropical maritime, with southeast trade winds. Hot, wet, humid summer, November–April; dry, cooler winter, May–October	Risk of heavy rain and cyclones during summer
Population	1.3 million (2010 estimate)	
Ethnic Makeup	Indo-Mauritian: 68% Creole: 27% Sino-Mauritian: 3% Franco-Mauritian: 2%	
Languages	English (de facto official language), French (business and media), Kreol (lingua franca), Bhojpuri, and other South and East Asian languages	
Religion	Hindu 48%; Roman Catholic 24%; other Christian 8%; Muslim 17%; other (including Buddhist) 3%	

Government	Parliamentary multiparty democracy based on Westminster model. Coalitions common. The president is head of state.	Nine mainland administrative districts and three dependencies (Rodrigues, Saint Brandon, and Agalega)
Currency	Mauritian rupee (Rs or MUR)	The exchange rate in 2010 was roughly Rs30 to US$1.
Media	MBC broadcasts national TV and radio. Also, local and international commercial channels	Free and democratic press, including *L'Express*, *Le Mauricien*, and *Week-End* (mostly in French)
Media: English-Language	*Mauritius Times* (weekly)	
Electricity	220 volts, 50 Hz	Both European two-prong (type C) and British three-prong (type G) plugs used. Power outages occur, especially during cyclones.
Weights and Measures	Generally metric, with some old French measurements still in use	Kilograms (kg) used in Western shops and supermarkets. Pounds (lb) often used at fruit and vegetable markets
Internet Domain	.mu	
Telephone	The country code for Mauritius is 230.	
Time Zone	GMT + 4 hours (+ 3 hours during British Summer Time)	

LAND &
PEOPLE

THE INDIAN OCEAN ISLANDS

Mauritius is a sovereign island nation in the
southwest Indian Ocean, which—together with
Réunion, Rodrigues, and the Cargados Carajos
Shoals—is one of the Mascarene Islands. Rodrigues is
a smaller island under Mauritian rule, approximately
350 miles (560 km) east of its larger neighbor. The
Cargados Carajos Shoals (also Mauritian) are located
some 267 miles (430 km) to the northeast of the
mainland. Réunion is a slightly larger but less
populous island ruled by France as a *département
d'outre-mer* (overseas department), and lies
approximately 135 miles (220 km) west of Mauritius.

The Mascarenes share a common geological
origin and natural history. They were formed by a
volcanic ridge that emerged some 8 to 10 million
years ago, which explains the strange rocks and
craters one finds on Mauritius, and the active
volcano on Réunion.

Alongside their Indian Ocean neighbors
Madagascar, the Seychelles, and the Comoros, these
islands have a shared history of slavery, colonialism
(under France or Britain), and maritime trade.
Looking further back and further afield, the islands
of the western Indian Ocean have been linked,
historically, to places as far-flung as East Africa, the

Arabian Peninsula, South and Southeast Asia, and beyond. As such, movements of people, goods, languages, and cultures have created a shared sense of belonging among the peoples of this part of the world. These days, many of the islands in the southwest Indian Ocean share a common bond in the French language.

GEOGRAPHY

The Republic of Mauritius (République de Maurice in French, Repiblik Moris in Kreol) comprises the main island of Mauritius and three dependencies: Rodrigues, the Cargados Carajos Shoals (or Saint Brandon), and the Agalega Islands. The country also holds territorial claims to Tromelin Island and the Chagos Archipelago, which are ruled, respectively, by France and the United Kingdom. The capital, Port Louis, is found in the northwest of

Mauritius. Administratively, the country is divided into nine mainland districts and three dependencies, which are subdivided into smaller municipalities.

Mauritius

The main island of Mauritius (Île Maurice), almost oval in shape and surrounded by coral reef, lies approximately 530 miles (855 km) east of

Madagascar in the southwest Indian Ocean. It is just north of the Tropic of Capricorn at 20° S, 57° E. A dot in the ocean measuring just 720 square miles (1,865 sq. km), it is about half the size of Rhode Island, or comparable to the English county of Buckinghamshire. Mauritius is renowned for its natural beauty, which led Mark Twain, who visited in 1896, to remark: "What there is of Mauritius is beautiful."

A coastline fringed with palms and casuarina trees, and measuring around 110 miles (177 km), rises sometimes steadily, sometimes steeply toward a central plateau at more than 1,300 feet (400 m). Though not nearly as rugged as neighboring Réunion, Mauritius is mountainous, with oddly shaped volcanic peaks dotting the interior of the island (Twain called them "quaint and picturesque groups of toy peaks"). The highest peak is Piton de la Petite Rivière Noire (2,717 feet, 828 m), followed closely by Pieter Both (2,690 feet, 820 m), Le Pouce (2,661 feet, 811 m), and Corps de Garde (2,362 feet, 720 m). Rivers, waterfalls, lakes, and reservoirs also occupy the interior, and the little

that remains of the once-pristine forest is now called the Black River Gorges National Park. The non-mountainous parts of the landscape are now dominated by endless fields of sugarcane.

The capital and main port, Port Louis (pronounced "por-looee" or "port-looiss"), is located in the northwest of Mauritius. Around 150,000 people (Port-Louisiens) live here, and many more travel to work here from other places on the island. Slightly further south, several towns have almost merged into one vast urban area within the Plaines Wilhems district (the central plateau towns, population approximately 400,000). These comprise, from northwest to southeast, Beau Bassin, Rose Hill (pronounced "roz-eel"), Quatre Bornes ("cat-born"), Vacoas ("vak-wa"), Phoénix ("fen-eeks"), and Curepipe ("cure-peep"), and are fast becoming the residential heartland of an urban middle class. Nowadays, they are popular among many expats who find Port Louis and other coastal areas to be too hot and humid. Mahébourg (pronounced "my-bor" or "my-burg," population 30,000) feels somewhat provincial in comparison, but has a popular market and historic sites related to Dutch settlement.

Rodrigues

At 40 square miles (104 sq. km), the younger island of Rodrigues is much smaller than Mauritius. Although hilly, its highest point, Mont Limon, reaches only 1,305 feet (398 m). Like Mauritius, Rodrigues (usually pronounced "rod-reeg" or "rod-reegs") is surrounded by lagoon and coral reef.
 It was initially visited by the Arabs, the Portuguese,

and the Dutch before being settled by the French and their African slaves in the eighteenth century, and then eventually seized by the British in 1809. Since October 2002, the Rodrigues Regional Assembly has enjoyed limited autonomy from Mauritius. The mostly Creole population stands at approximately 38,000 (2010), living mainly in the sleepy capital Port Mathurin and some other small settlements. Life is quieter than on Mauritius, and Rodrigues has yet to feel the effects of mass tourism. Employment is mainly in fishing and small-scale farming. With an early-to-bed, early-to-rise culture, many businesses close before 4:00 p.m.

Cargados Carajos Shoals (Saint Brandon)
The Cargados Carajos Shoals (commonly known as Saint Brandon) lie some 267 miles (430 km) northeast of Mauritius. They consist of a few dozen scattered sandbanks, shoals, rocks, and islets within 73 square miles (190 sq. km) of reef, protecting important flora and marine life. A small, non-permanent community of Mauritians works mainly in the fishing industry.

MAURITIAN PLACE-NAMES

Mauritian history and its diverse ethnic makeup are evident in the place-names that dot the country's landscape: names like Flacq and Plaines Wilhems bear witness to the Dutch presence in the sixteenth century; Port Louis and Mahébourg pay homage to former French monarchs and governors; some places have distinctly British-sounding names like Highlands and Rose Hill; and others remind us of former military posts, sugar plantations, and colonial residences (Quartier Militaire and Quatre Bornes, for instance).

Many names are more exotic, like Surinam, Sébastopol, Yemen, and Médine (Medina), and others tell us of the Hindu presence on the island: Gokoola, Coromandel, Bénarès (the French spelling of Banaras or Varanasi), and Ganga Talao (Grand Bassin in French), to mention just a few. Names of mountains and rivers can sometimes seem quite literal in comparison, but are nonetheless quite entertaining: take, for example, Le Pouce Mountain, with its thumblike shape, Rivière Noire (Black River), Blue Bay (as it says on the tin), and Lion Mountain (from Mahébourg it looks like the Sphinx).

Agalega Islands

Agalega is made up of two islands with a total area of 9 square miles (24 sq. km), which can be found 700 miles (1,100 km) north of Mauritius, near the Seychelles. Here, the three hundred or so inhabitants work in fishing and coconut exploitation.

Chagos Archipelago (Disputed Territory)

The Chagos Archipelago is a group of around sixty-five islands in the center of the Indian Ocean, approximately 1,000 miles (1,600 km) south of India and 1,200 miles (1,930 km) northeast of Mauritius. Originally settled by Franco-Mauritians and their African and Malagasy slaves in the eighteenth century, and then also by south Indian laborers, the islands once thrived on coconut plantations. They are currently ruled as an overseas territory of the United Kingdom as the British Indian Ocean Territory (BIOT).

In the mid-1960s, perhaps as a bargain for Mauritian independence, negotiations were held between the United Kingdom and the Mauritian Council of Ministers over the future of the Chagos islands, which were eventually detached from Mauritius in 1965. The largest island, Diego Garcia, was leased to the USA to build a strategic (and secretive) military base in the early 1970s. The issues surrounding this have become hugely controversial, and in recent years many commentators, as well as the Mauritian government, have claimed that the Chagos islands were ceded illegally from the country.

Meanwhile, the plight of the native Chagossians (Îlois) has become increasingly prominent. More than 1,500 islanders were forcibly removed to Mauritius (and smaller numbers to the Seychelles) between 1968 and 1973, and many have since lived a poor and marginalized existence on the outskirts of Port Louis. Others settled in Britain. The situation has created a major diplomatic rift between the Chagossians and Mauritius on the one hand, and the UK and the USA on the other. The Chagos Refugees Group, which campaigns on behalf of exiled islanders, had some success when the British High Court ruled in 2000 and 2006 that their expulsion was unlawful; no effective right of return has been offered, however. A case at the European Court of Human Rights was pending in 2010. It seems likely that a settlement will be agreed upon, allowing the Chagossians at least to return to visit the graves of their ancestors.

Tromelin (Disputed Territory)

A very small (0.38 sq. miles, 1 sq. km), largely inaccessible island located between Mauritius and northern Madagascar, Tromelin (Île Tromelin) has been a French overseas territory (*territoire d'outre-mer*) since the 1950s. Nonetheless, the island is claimed by Mauritius, and Madagascar and the Seychelles also have designs on it. The status of Tromelin was already unclear when the British took control of Mauritius in 1810 (the translation and finer semantics of the 1814 Treaty of Paris are found somewhat wanting). The island is now the site of an important French cyclone monitoring station. In 2009, France and Mauritius agreed to share the management of Tromelin's natural habitat and fishing waters.

CLIMATE AND WEATHER

Mauritius has a tropical maritime climate. There are two marked seasons: a hot, wet, and humid summer between November and April, and a dry, cooler winter between May and October. Average temperatures are 68.7°F (20.4°C) in winter and 76.5°F (24.7°C) in summer, though many coastal areas experience temperatures far higher than this (sometimes as high as 97°F/36°C in January and February). The year-round sunshine is tempered by southeast trade winds and heavy showers.

Temperatures tend to be cooler as you head inland to the central plateau, and the wettest weather is found in the area from Curepipe to the southeast of the island (typically from January to March, but also at other times of year).

During summer, the country is at risk of tropical cyclones. There is a cyclone warning system to prevent destruction and loss of life (from class 1 to class 4). If four red flags are raised above public buildings and the media warns of a class 4 cyclone (winds over 75 mph/120 kmph), the population is advised to stay indoors.

There is increasing concern among Mauritians over climatic conditions in the Indian Ocean, especially in relation to global warming. Some commentators suggest that global warming has affected the local climate by causing an overall decrease in local rainfall, accompanied by heavier showers and flash floods in summer months.

THE PEOPLE
According to a government report in 2010, Mauritius has a population of 1,281,214. Considering its small size, and the use of large swathes of land for growing sugarcane (over a third of the land), it is among the most densely populated countries in the world, at 1,626 people per square mile (628 per sq. km).

Town and Country
Historically, there have always been huge differences between the lives of Mauritians living in the towns (more than 40 percent of the population) and those living in rural areas. Settlements in urban areas range from slums and high-rise apartments to modest single-story with gardens, yards, and driveways. Low-rise, concrete accommodation is more common due to the threat of cyclones. Wealthy Mauritians sometimes own larger houses and, increasingly, vacation homes by the sea (known locally as a *bungalow* or *kanpman*).

Rural areas are still characterized by a largely Indo-Mauritian population, living in small villages and estates surrounding the centers of the sugar industry in the island's north and northeast. After emancipation, Creoles settled in fishing villages, particularly in the traditional Creole heartland of the southwest (Black River District). With a diversified economy and a more mobile, better educated population, however, all this is beginning to change.

Ethnic Categories

There is no indigenous population. Mauritians are a mixed people whose ancestors had their roots in many places around the world. The country has sometimes been called a "United Nations in miniature." Most islanders are the descendants of Africans, Malagasies, Europeans, South Asians, or Chinese, or any combination of these groups, who settled here from the early eighteenth century.

The population is normally categorized in terms of distinct ethno-religious groups: Hindus and Muslims (traditionally known together as Indo-Mauritians), Creoles, Sino-Mauritians, and Franco-Mauritians. To a large extent, and despite official pronouncements, Mauritian society is effectively organized and divided along the lines of ethnicity, religion, and language. As a result, a growing sense of disharmony has accompanied the newfound dominance of the majority Hindus in public life.

Hindus

Hindus in Mauritius make up around half the population. They are widely perceived to be the group that dominates the public sector and, alongside the old Franco-Mauritian elite, occupies many high-ranking positions in the private sector. This is, however, a relatively new phenomenon: Hindus, and Indo-Mauritians in general, were largely disadvantaged and politically disenfranchised until the postwar years and the coming of independence in 1968.

The Hindus have been successful in continuing many of the religious and cultural traditions of their ancestors, and sacrifice, family connections, and kinship are central to their lives. Great pains have been taken to cultivate cultural and religious links with Hindus and Hindu organizations in India. Hindu pride, and sometimes nationalism, can be seen in the numerous statues of deities and red flags found outside homes across the island.

A simplified, hereditary caste system (*jati*) exists among Mauritian Hindus, whereby members of the Babuji-Maraz (Brahmin high caste, dominant in the Hindu priesthood), the Vaish (middle caste, perceived to be the dominant caste in government and state administration), the Gahlot Rajput (low caste), and the Ravived (also low caste) have traditionally kept themselves to themselves. However, rapid social change and intermarriage have weakened the caste system.

Many are unaware of the cultural, linguistic, and geographical backgrounds of Mauritian Hindus. A family name is often used as a way of guessing the background of another Indo-Mauritian (or any Mauritian, for that matter).

Biharis

Around 80 percent of Mauritian Hindus are known as Biharis, meaning they are the descendants of northeastern Indian immigrants. These forebears arrived in Mauritius from the mid-nineteenth century as indentured laborers from the states of Bihar and Uttar Pradesh. Biharis are known to be politically and culturally dominant among Hindus on the island.

Tamils

Mauritian Tamils are the descendants of immigrants from what is now Tamil Nadu in southern India. Many helped to build the island's original infrastructure and bought land and sugar estates in the nineteenth century. They generally follow the Hindu tradition, but some have converted to Christianity and other religions. Today Tamils make up more than 6 percent of the population, and they hold considerable social and cultural importance.

Telugus

Telugus originally arrived in Mauritius from the Andhra Pradesh area of southern India and now make up around 3 percent of the population. Intermarriage with other Hindus and conversions to Christianity have broken down the traditional Telugu community. There have, however, been moves to revive the Telugu language and traditions, and the Telugu New Year, Ougadi, is celebrated with passion.

Marathis

Marathis are the descendants of indentured laborers and artisans from Maharashtra in western and central India. They make up around 2 percent of the population of the island.

Creoles

Creoles make up around 27 percent of the Mauritian population and are largely the descendants of African and Malagasy slaves, though many are actually of mixed African,

Malagasy, South Asian, European, and Chinese ancestry. Even so, in relation to Indo-, Franco-, and Sino-Mauritians, Creoles often lack a clear sense of continuity between their ancestors and their lives in modern Mauritius. Unlike in some other parts of the world, there is little in the way of black consciousness among Mauritian Creoles, although many are involved in cultural activism. Rastafarianism has also been developing in recent decades as a subculture influenced by Caribbean cultural and musical traditions.

Creoles have often been caricatured as fun-loving, irresponsible, and individualistic, lacking in morals and a sense of purpose. The stereotype also suggests that they live for the present, frittering their money away on idle pursuits. Such racism fails to see the enormous diversity in the Creole population, however, and there are many successful Mauritians of a Creole background.

Predominantly Roman Catholic, the Creoles have historically formed a sizeable working class and have often been the poorest of the island's population. This has recently bred resentment *vis-à-vis* the Hindu-dominated administration. Poorer Afro-Mauritian Creoles largely live in the southwest of the island and in slums on the outskirts of Port Louis, though a socially mobile and influential middle class has developed in the central plateau towns.

Muslims
Muslims make up around 17 percent of the population. They are largely the descendants of Gujarati merchants and sailors, and indentured laborers from northeast India. A small number of

Creoles and Hindu Mauritians have also converted to Islam. Traditional Mauritian Muslims tend to rely on family and ancestral ties in their daily and professional lives, and they are reputed to be sober, industrious, and religiously devoted. The local *jamaat* (Islamic council or organization) plays an important role in the life of the community.

Despite becoming wealthy through trade (notably in textiles and foodstuffs) and employment in the professions, some Muslims see themselves as a besieged minority on a Hindu-dominated island, but Islamic fundamentalism is certainly not as strong here as in other parts of the world. Nevertheless, rich and poor Muslims on the island are extremely proud of their origins and traditions. The Port Louis suburb of Plaine Verte and parts of Vacoas are the areas with the largest concentration of Muslims, although many also live in rural areas.

Sino-Mauritians

Most Sino-Mauritians are the descendants of free immigrants who left to escape poverty and hardship in China from the late nineteenth century onward; smaller numbers had arrived as indentured laborers at earlier stages in Mauritian history. Many are Cantonese and Fukienese, but the majority belong to the Hakka ethnic group.

Sino-Mauritians quickly established themselves as successful retailers, and many local shops in towns and villages are still owned by Sino-Mauritian families. The community, some 40,000 strong (3 percent of the population) and based largely in Chinatown in Port Louis and in some of the central plateau towns, relies on a patriarchal family unit and clan system for mutual support, although intermarriage and social change mean it is now better integrated into general Mauritian society. Sino-Mauritians are known to be hardworking and are an increasingly prosperous component of the Mauritian elite.

Franco-Mauritians

Forming less than 2 percent of the population, there are fewer than 25,000 Franco-Mauritians on the island. Many are the descendants of aristocrats who fled the French Revolution, while others are the descendants of an assortment of sailors, farmers, convicts, and slave owners who made up the original French colonists. Some British, Irish, and other European settlers have, over the years, been integrated into this community. Historically, Franco-Mauritians owned huge areas of land across the island; they now form a small, wealthy, and somewhat insular group, holding many important positions in the private sector, particularly the sugar industry and banking. They have continued to follow French traditions and often live in spacious, well-guarded homes in the central plateau towns. Before and since independence—possibly fearing the political ascent of other communities—many Franco-Mauritians emigrated to France, Australia, and South Africa.

Mauritians Around the World

Labor migration since the 1960s and the increasing number of Mauritians moving abroad for university education have meant that large numbers of Mauritians can be found in French- and English-speaking countries around the world. Although difficult to quantify and usually well integrated in their host communities, these expatriates have a sense of pride in being Mauritian, and many have maintained their Mauritian language and culture.

In the United Kingdom, communities can be found in south and north London (Tottenham is known as "Little Mauritius") and other large cities like Birmingham, Cardiff, and Glasgow. France is home to large numbers of emigrants, mainly in Paris and in Strasbourg, where there is a Tamil community. Others have settled in Belgium, Switzerland, Italy, the Netherlands, and the Scandinavian countries. There has also been a long presence of Franco-Mauritians and other groups in Australia, particularly in Melbourne. In the early years of the twentieth century South Africa welcomed many Creoles and Franco-Mauritians to work in the Natal sugar industry, and there are currently small communities in Durban and Cape Town. Canada, which, like Mauritius, has ties to the French and English languages, is home to Mauritian communities in Montreal, Toronto, and Vancouver. Finally, many more Mauritians have moved abroad to India, the Middle East, and— closer to home—Réunion for work and study.

A BRIEF HISTORY

Mauritius was first settled only around four hundred years ago. Although Mauritian society has undergone major upheavals and transformations throughout its short history from the early sixteenth century to the present day, its development has been characterized more by evolution than by revolution. Slavery was abolished gradually, as was the indenture system, and Mauritius moved toward becoming a republic over a protracted period of several decades. In Mauritius, history has progressed in a series of slow, sure steps, at each moment involving disagreement and eventual compromise between the different parties involved. What has emerged out of this is a stable, multiparty democracy and a relative social and economic success story.

Pre-Colonization

The precolonial history of Mauritius is shrouded in mystery and doubt, but it seems that an uninhabited Mauritius was first visited by Arabs and perhaps South and Southeast Asian sailors at various points up until the twelfth century. The Arabs, arriving by dhow, named the island Diva Harab (Desert Island, usually known in its European corrupted form Dina Arobi). When they arrived—there are no clear records other than the geographer Al Idrissi's twelfth-century maps—the island probably displayed an unspoiled natural environment that had evolved in isolation for millennia.

After a hiatus of a few centuries, Portuguese sailors arrived in the first decades of the sixteenth century, headed by Diogo Fernandes Pereira in 1507. The islands first began to appear on European maritime charts during this period, and the Portuguese named Mauritius Ilha do Cirne (Swan Island), probably after Pereira's ship *Cirne*. Although they left little concrete evidence of their visits, Portuguese influence lives on in the names of some locations, chiefly the Mascarenes and Rodrigues (after the explorers Pedro Mascarenhas and Diogo Rodrigues). After brief visits to Cirne, the Portuguese left without settling the island.

The Dutch Arrival

With news of this "discovery" and their maritime power in the ascendant, Dutch sailors began visiting the Mascarenes in the late sixteenth century. Under the aegis of the Dutch East India Company, a fleet of ships arrived on September 20, 1598, and named their new possession after the Dutch ruler Prince Maurits van Nassau (1567–1625). They found traces of earlier visits and nonnative flora and fauna, but it was these new settlers themselves who were to transform the island beyond repair.

Early Dutch accounts of Mauritius mention the initial sight of dense forest, huge tortoises, and a strange, waddling bird—the famous dodo. These settlers decided to log the native forest for valuable ebony, and imported an assortment of nonnative animals (rats, pigs, monkeys, goats, cows, Java deer, and poultry), foreign spices, tobacco, and sugar. Human activity would eventually wipe out many native animals like the dodo.

Even from its earliest settlement, Mauritius was a multicultural place. The Dutch brought an assortment of other Europeans with them to the island, and slaves and convicts were forcibly moved to Mauritius from as far afield as Africa, Madagascar, Southeast Asia, and Southern India.

After failing to set up a viable colony between 1638 and 1658, the Dutch started afresh in 1664. Despite finding life on this remote island very difficult, they developed a port in a natural harbor in the southeast, improved the infrastructure, and increased exports of ebony and ambergris. Mauritius also functioned as a strategic base for the Dutch East India Company, which operated its trade on a vast scale across the Indian Ocean and beyond. Nonetheless, cyclones, rats, and an unmanageable population of rebellious slaves and convicts eventually finished off the Dutch project. They finally gave up and left for good in 1710.

The French
French ships had already visited Mauritius to exploit its natural resources and to stop for rest on their way to trading ports in India. They had also settled and set up coffee plantations on nearby Isle Bourbon

(now Réunion) in the latter part of the seventeenth century. Just five years after the Dutch had departed, the French East India Company claimed Mauritius on behalf of the French crown, renaming it Isle de France. Settlement began in 1721, with a governor, Lazarist priests, and a few French families (who arrived from Isle Bourbon with their slaves) eventually making it their home. The French would control the island for the next century, continuing to bring people from far and wide, both as free laborers and as slaves.

Meanwhile, French Huguenot refugees led by François Leguat had settled on nearby Rodrigues (uninhabited and still free from Catholic French control) in around 1691, but soon left after failing to turn the island into a viable home.

Slaves were their owners' property, and extreme violence was used to subjugate them. Under the authority of the French *Code Noir*, slaves were initially brought from Madagascar, but later also from southern India and East and West Africa. They initially worked the land, cultivating rice, wheat, and tobacco, and later developed the sugar industry. Many escaped and lived in the mountains and forests of the island, leading to brutal maroon hunts (*chasses aux marrons*). (See page 77.)

For several decades the island was used as a strategic base for attacking British ships heading for India, and to protect Isle Bourbon and the newly acquired French Indian territories in Pondicherry and Madras. The main port and trade hub was transferred from the southeast to the northwest, to the present capital, Port Louis. Mahé de Labourdonnais, who became governor in 1735, is credited with developing the island's infrastructure, including hospitals, coastal fortifications, a new harbor, stores, and government buildings. In this same year, France created a permanent farming colony in Rodrigues, which was settled by Frenchmen and their slaves.

In 1767, the French East India Company sold Isle de France to the French crown, which now had direct administrative control. By now the island was firmly established in the imaginations of the French and other Europeans as a tropical idyll, as suggested by Bernardin de St. Pierre in his tragic, romantic novel, *Paul et Virginie* (1787). Under intendant Pierre Poivre, agriculture was intensified and individual French settlers were encouraged to trade more freely in goods and slaves in the Indian Ocean. Plantation slavery had become firmly entrenched on the island, and a small elite of Franco-Mauritians had established itself as a group whose *raison d'être* was to profit from sugar and slavery.

The British
Despite the distant French Revolution causing fear and unrest among the Franco-Mauritians, slavery persisted. French-allied privateers also

continued to disrupt the business of the rival British East India Company, increasing the likelihood of full-scale war in the Indian Ocean. In 1810, during the Napoleonic Wars, the British at first failed at Grand Port and then succeeded in capturing a vulnerable Isle de France (under the command of General Decaen) at Cap Malheureux. The new rulers reverted to using its former name, Mauritius. They also added Rodrigues, the Seychelles and—briefly—Réunion to their booty, and the Treaty of Paris (1814) guaranteed Britain's control of the Indian Ocean.

The British did not disturb the delicate balance of power on the island, however, and the Franco-Mauritian elite was allowed to retain its laws, customs, and the Catholic religion. The few British families who settled on the island were soon assimilated into the Franco-Mauritian aristocracy. On a visit to Mauritius in 1836, Charles Darwin remarked: "I should think that Calais or Boulogne was much more Anglified."

Slavery was abolished in 1835, and the Franco-Mauritians were compensated with huge payments.

An apprenticeship system tied the freed slaves to their former masters for several years, but many refused this humiliation and settled the coastal areas of Mauritius—as far away as possible from the plantations—to earn their living from fishing, farming, and local trade.

Indentured Labor

Following abolition, new ways were sought to fill the labor shortage and the colonial system of indenture was implemented to lure hundreds of thousands of laborers ("coolies") from regions near the major ports of the Indian subcontinent. Some of these immigrants returned to their homelands, while others arrived independently to work as traders and skilled craftsmen. Laborers were housed in basic huts alongside the sugar plantations, followed strict rules, and were closely monitored by *sirdars* (fellow Indians employed as overseers). The indenture system—which has been called a "new system of slavery" by historian Hugh Tinker— lasted right up until 1924, and left a lasting impression on Mauritian society. The island would henceforth be characterized by a large majority of Indo-Mauritians, and the population would increase dramatically from 62,000 in 1810 to 370,000 in 1901.

A malaria epidemic in the 1860s caused an exodus from densely populated Port Louis toward the cooler, healthier climate of the central plateau, creating new towns and villages in the process. The social, economic, and sanitary conditions of Indian laborers were still very poor at the turn of the century: Mahatma Gandhi visited Mauritius in 1901 and witnessed their plight, and arranged for lawyer Manilal Doctor to establish himself on the island to ensure their welfare. Meanwhile, many aspiring immigrants had slowly become farmers themselves, buying land off cash-strapped Franco-Mauritians. Indo-Mauritians and Creoles were, however, largely excluded from the island's newly developing political system, into which the British had co-opted the Franco-Mauritian elite.

The Mauritian Labour Party was formed by Dr. Maurice Curé in 1936, and strikes and protests were organized in favor of labor and voting rights for the masses. Political reforms and enfranchisement in the postwar years—including universal suffrage in 1959—resulted in the ascent of an Indo-Mauritian elite that still exists today. In the following decades, free universal education (from 1976), health care, housing, democracy, and pensions were developed, improving the lot of the Mauritian population.

Independence

The increasingly educated and politicized population had now become a force to be reckoned with, and a deal to cede the Chagos Archipelago from mainland Mauritius in 1965 gave the emergent Indo-Mauritian political brokers greater leverage in their campaign for Mauritian self-governance. Following hotly contested elections (seen locally as a referendum on self-rule), Mauritius gained independence from the United Kingdom on March 12, 1968, although many Creoles, Muslims, and Franco- and Sino-Mauritians wanted British rule to continue.

Nevertheless, a new nation was born and the first prime minister, Sir Seewoosagur Ramgoolam, was proclaimed "Father of the Nation."

In the years following independence, Mauritius, now largely under the control of the Indo-Mauritian elite, at first suffered overpopulation and chronic unemployment. It then began a course of radical economic and social change, moving away from a sugar monocrop economy toward diversification based on textiles, tourism, and the service industry. With encouragement and loans from the International Monetary Fund and the World Bank, a campaign of liberalization was launched and an export processing zone encouraged greater international trade. Unemployment was cut drastically and women became more prominent in the labor market. From a situation of relative poverty, Mauritius had become one of the most promising newly developed nations in the world, an "economic miracle" and the "tiger of the Indian Ocean."

In 1992, the country took a further step away from Britain by becoming a republic (the Queen had previously been head of state), but chose to retain its ties through continued membership of the Commonwealth.

Despite its seemingly stable and democratic nature, interethnic tensions grew. Left-wing parties such as the Mouvement Militant

Mauricien (MMM) were formed to challenge the hegemony of the Hindu Mauritian elite. Riots were a common occurrence in the late 1960s (a hundred people died in Muslim–Creole riots in January 1968) and resurfaced in the late 1990s. In 1999, a popular Creole musician called Kaya (real name Joseph Réginald Topize) was arrested while allegedly smoking cannabis at a rally. He later died in police custody, sparking interethnic riots across the island and shattering the myth of Mauritius as an island of peaceful coexistence. To many, this was an inevitable consequence of the marginalization of poor Creoles by the newly dominant Hindu state machinery. Unless the government can deal effectively with pockets of poverty on the outskirts of Port Louis and racism toward Afro-Mauritians, social problems look set to be a characteristic of Mauritian society for years to come.

All things considered, Mauritians today are increasingly affluent, especially when compared with other countries in the wider African and Indian Ocean region. Many can now afford to own cars and their own homes, and their spending power would be unimaginable to those who toiled in the sugarcane fields a generation or two ago.

GOVERNMENT AND POLITICS
Mauritius is still a relatively young democracy, there having been only nine general elections since independence in 1968.

SOME KEY DATES

Tenth–twelfth centuries Arab and South/Southeast Asian sailors visit the Mascarene Islands.

1507 Portuguese sailors visit and possibly stay on the island of Mauritius.

1528 Neighboring Rodrigues is discovered by Portuguese navigator Diogo Rodrigues.

1598 Dutch sailors arrive, naming Mauritius in honor of Prince Maurits of Nassau. They begin to destroy the natural habitat and wipe out the indigenous dodo.

1638 The Dutch establish a permanent presence on Mauritius.

1710 The Dutch give up their colony and leave Mauritius.

1715 The French East India Company claims the island as crown territory, naming it Isle de France.

1735 Mahé de Labourdonnais is nominated governor of the Mascarenes, subsequently improving the infrastructure of the colony.

1767 Power is transferred directly to the French crown. Slavery is intensified and sugar plantations subsequently become the basis of the island's economy.

1787 Publication of Bernardin de St. Pierre's *Paul et Virginie*, set in Mauritius.

1809 The British seize the island of Rodrigues.

1810 The British capture Isle de France, hereafter known as Mauritius (Île Maurice in French).

1814 Treaty of Paris is signed, transferring Mauritius to the British crown.

1835 Slavery is abolished in British colonies and indentured labor is intensified.

1860s Disease and squalor cause many islanders to leave Port Louis for the cooler, healthier central plateau

1901 Mahatma Gandhi visits Mauritius, staying in Port Louis. Upon returning to India, he sends Manilal Doctor to Mauritius to ensure the welfare of Indian laborers.

1965 Chagos islands are detached from Mauritius by the United Kingdom, to be used later as an American military base.

1968 Mauritius gains independence from the United Kingdom on March 12, led by Sir Seewoosagur Ramgoolam. There are interethnic riots and social unrest.

1992 Mauritius proclaims itself a republic within the Commonwealth.

1999 Death in custody of Kaya, a famous Creole musician, results in interethnic riots.

2002 Rodrigues achieves regional autonomy from Mauritius.

2003 Franco-Mauritian Paul Bérenger becomes the country's first non-Indo-Mauritian prime minister.

2005 Navin Ramgoolam wins election to become prime minister.

2010 Ramgoolam elected for a second term of five years.

In 2010, the president was Sir Anerood Jugnauth (since 2003) and the prime minister was Dr. Navin Ramgoolam (since 2005). A lively, open, multiparty democracy functions well in this country, leading to a liberal society in which there is a combination of a welfare state and a strong private-sector economy.

The general public has a healthy appetite for politics—voter turnout usually exceeds 75 percent. Politics can sometimes be an acrimonious affair, however, where class, caste, and ethnic allegiances often matter more to voters than genuine political concerns, and resentment toward Hindu politicians has grown among Creoles and Muslims. Shifting coalitions and allegiances are followed by bitter disagreements, and a dynastic form of politics means that it is common for close family to follow relatives into particular political parties (the Ramgoolam, Jugnauth, and Duval families, for instance). In spite of this, the National Assembly demands a courteous and polite approach toward one's adversaries. As in other areas of public life, Mauritian politics is dominated by men.

Parliamentary System

Mauritian government broadly follows the Westminster model, with members of parliament voted into the unicameral National Assembly in first-past-the-post general elections held every five years. Since the country became a republic in 1992, the incumbent president has been the official head of state, although his role is largely that of an honorary, nonexecutive constitutional figurehead. The president's official residence is a sumptuous mansion called Le Château de Réduit, near Rose Hill, with an accompanying 240 acres (97 hectares) of land.

The prime minister of the republic, leader of the majority party or coalition, wields executive power and forms a cabinet. His official residence is Clarisse House in Vacoas-Phoénix.

The National Assembly—which convenes in an amphitheater-style room at the historic eighteenth-century Government House in Port Louis—comprises 70 members, 62 of whom are elected directly by 21 constituencies. The remaining eight members are nominated by the Electoral Supervisory Commission as part of a "best loser" system, ensuring that all ethnic and religious groups are represented.

Local government is organized into city, municipal, district, and village councils, which consist of elected councilors. The role of local government is to provide services and amenities to the Mauritian population.

Major Political Parties

The main political parties are the Parti Travailliste (Mauritian Labour Party, largely supported by Hindus), the Mouvement Socialiste Militant (Militant Socialist Movement, MSM, also competing for the Hindu vote), the Mouvement Militant Mauricien (Mauritian Militant Movement, MMM, multiethnic, but popular among Creoles and Muslims), and the Parti Mauricien Social Démocrate (Mauritian Social Democratic Party, PMSD).

Recent Political History

Since independence, Mauritian politics has been characterized by a number of coalitions between the major political parties. "Father of the Nation" Sir Seewoosagur Ramgoolam and his Labour-led coalition ruled from 1968 until 1982, followed by Anerood Jugnauth and his Mauritian Socialist Party (later renamed the MSM) from 1982 until 1995, with the help of various coalitions (notably with Paul Bérenger's MMM in 1982–3). Dr. Navinchandra (Navin) Ramgoolam, son of Sir Seewoosagur Ramgoolam, regained power for the Labour Party in a coalition with the MMM in 1995, but elections in 2000 saw an MSM–MMM coalition emerge victorious amid accusations of corruption leveled at Labour ministers. Sir Anerood Jugnauth led as prime minister from 2000 until 2003, followed by Franco-Mauritian Paul Bérenger (2003–5), the country's first non-Indo-Mauritian prime minister. From 2005, Mauritians have once again been ruled by Labour-led coalitions under Navin Ramgoolam.

The general elections in 2010 saw the victory of the Alliance de l'Avenir (Coalition for the Future, comprising Labour, the PMSD, and the MSM). Ramgoolam, a Dublin- and London-educated doctor and lawyer, pledged to continue to encourage foreign investment and diversify the economy in the wake of the world financial crisis.

Several presidents have held office since the country became a republic in 1992, notably Sir Anerood Jugnauth (2003–) and Mauritian Muslim Cassam Uteem (between 1992 and 2002), the longest-serving president so far. Uteem resigned in opposition to a controversial antiterrorism law introduced after the 9/11 attacks in New York.

Law

The Mauritian constitution enshrines the separation of powers, meaning that the judiciary (including the Mauritius Supreme Court) is independent. The legal system is a combination of the French Napoleonic Code and English Common Law. Appeals can be made to the Judicial Committee of the Privy Council in the UK.

TRADE AND INTERNATIONAL RELATIONS

The Mauritian economy is based on three main industries: textiles, sugar, and tourism. In addition to these sectors, tertiary service industries such as offshore banking and call centers are becoming increasingly important in island life.

Manufacturing has developed in the main urban areas. Foreign investment and tourism seem to be key areas of future growth, and around a million tourists visit the island each year, many from South Africa and wealthy European countries. Another project for the future is to expand upon Cyber City

(the island's own Silicon Valley, built in Ébène in 2004), making Mauritius a location of choice for the software development, data storage, and high-tech industries.

The country's principal trading partners are France, South Africa, the United Kingdom, and India. The United Kingdom is the destination of around 30 percent of Mauritian exports, principally sugar and clothing, and the United States receives around 9 percent of total exports. The export processing zone established in 1971 is now the largest employer on the island, and women make up around 70 percent of its workforce.

The recent global recession took its time to reach Mauritius, but the country has suffered a marked decrease in revenue from tourism. The government controlled the effects of the recession by pumping hundreds of millions of dollars into the economy.

Through membership of the Commonwealth and La Francophonie, and special agreements with the European Union, Mauritius has maintained close ties with its two former colonial powers. The country is also a member of the Southern African Development Community, offering advantageous trade agreements and tax benefits, as well as the African Union, the Common Market of Eastern and Southern Africa, the Indian Ocean Commission, and the Indian Ocean Rim–Association for Regional Cooperation. Double taxation avoidance agreements exist between Mauritius and a number of other countries.

THE DODO

The dodo has been the subject of a lot of misinformation since people first set eyes upon it in Mauritius in the sixteenth century. According to one theory, upon seeing a plump, waddling, flightless bird, the Portuguese had initially named it the *doudo*, emphasizing their perception of a foolish and crazy creature. The Dutch would later call it the *walghvogel*, a disgusting bird, partly because of the taste of its tough flesh. Later still, European paintings and engravings would caricature the bird and accentuate its odd features, and the dodo would make a cameo appearance in Lewis Carroll's *Alice's Adventures in Wonderland*. Nowadays, it is a symbol of stupidity and extinction at the hands of destructive human beings.

Since it had no predators on the island, the dodo had lived a happy, carefree existence until the Europeans arrived. The Dutch settlers at first amused themselves by chasing the slow-moving dodos and hitting them with sticks, before discovering that the flesh could provide hearty meals for large groups of sailors. Nonnative animals such as monkeys, cats, and dogs would also feast on the bird, since it was easy to catch and provided an excellent

source of protein. Within a hundred years of its discovery, the dodo was erased from the face of the planet. By 1681 it was dead as a dodo.

Dodology, the study of the natural history of this bird, has developed in its absence. The dodo, or *Raphus cucullatus*, was closely related to the dove and the pigeon. Reconstructions suggest that it was a few feet tall (roughly the size of a swan), with gray plumage, small, white wings and a large, hooked bill. Due to an absence of predators and its isolation on the island, the dodo became larger and lost its ability to fly. Its eggs were left defenseless in nests on the ground. It became extinct in large part due to this vulnerability; this was a similar story to that of the "white dodo" on Réunion and the longer-necked solitaire on Rodrigues, which were also ill prepared for the arrival of humans and other animals.

The dodo fed on fruit, nuts, seeds, and snails, using a tough beak adapted to this diet. Due to its size and feeding habits, one commentator has referred to the bird, somewhat disparagingly, as the "avian equivalent of pigs and goats."

The dodo is now a potent symbol of the lost innocence of Mauritius, and is one of the only things one can claim to be native to the island; almost everything else—humans, other animals, languages, religions, foods, sugar, and spices—was introduced from elsewhere. As we shall see, this lack of an indigenous culture and tradition has been a defining aspect of Mauritian history.

VALUES &
ATTITUDES

Mauritians are generally assumed to be very
gregarious and extroverted, but their friendliness
is actually tempered by a polite reserve. Much, of
course, depends on each individual's background
(Creoles are reputed to be the most sociable,
Indo-Mauritians less so), but you may notice that
many islanders will give you a little distance when
first meeting you. Nevertheless, once they get to
know you, they can be touchingly warm and will
go out of their way to help you. Diplomacy,
compromise, and pragmatism are common traits,
as are courtesy, respect, and being *bien élevé*
(having good manners).

TOLERANCE AND DIVERSITY

Mauritians are warm, polite, and respectful
people who are tolerant of diversity. In fact,
multiculturalism *is* the culture of Mauritius.
However, although tourist brochures promoting
a "rainbow island" would have you believe
otherwise, you are not likely to encounter perfect
harmony. Rather, it is an unspoken rule that
Mauritians acknowledge the cultural and religious
diversity of their compatriots. Since they live on
an island, there's not much else they can do but

accept the nature of their society, respect their compatriots, and get on with life. As a result people have an impressive understanding of and respect for each other's religions and traditions. Born of necessity, this multiculturalism is a major component of their national identity

HOSPITALITY AND MEETING FOREIGNERS

Mauritians have a reputation for hospitality toward foreigners. This could well be a result of the island's history as a stop-off point for people traveling (or being forcibly moved) around the Indian Ocean, as well as an expression of the cultural traditions of its population. The infectious Mauritian smile says it all. Matthew Flinders, an early nineteenth-century British navigator, despite being arrested upon arrival by the French authorities, was not insensitive to the charms of the Mauritians; he wrote: ". . . never, in any place, or amongst any people, have I seen more hospitality and attention to strangers— more sensibility to the misfortunes of others, of whatever nation, than here."

Quite unsurprisingly, one of the things that Mauritians do best is tourism, which allows them to demonstrate their welcoming nature. Most Mauritians love their island and would be proud to show you their country and its rich heritage.

BEING MAURITIAN

The people of Mauritius are still trying to define the nature of *le mauricianisme*, or "Mauritianness," and this is largely due to the relative infancy of their society and the plural nature of its population. Mauritians generally look in one of two directions for their sense of identity: to the homelands of their ancestors in different parts of the world, or to the cultural kaleidoscope of the island, where a hybrid culture can be seen as an inventive way of creating cultural cohesion.

Competing ideas of Mauritian identity have come to the fore in recent decades as the more socially conservative Hindus have excelled in the political arena at the expense of the Creoles. Creoles, who generally take a more positive view of mixing, have become socially, economically, and politically marginalized. As a solution, many modern Mauritians propose a new approach, "unity in diversity," stressing the pluralism of the island as its defining feature. Thus, there is a growing sense of an island identity free from specific ethnic allegiances.

THE IMPORTANCE OF FAMILY

Family is a fundamental institution in Mauritian society. Although the extent to which family matters varies between the communities (Creole families tend to be less closely knit than Indo-Mauritians, for example), it is common for Mauritians of all backgrounds to keep in close contact with their extended family. This might mean just attending important family rites of passage such as birthdays, weddings, and other celebrations, or—more traditionally—living with three generations under one roof or sharing a common yard or driveway. Today it is still common for young adults to live with their parents until they get married, if only for financial reasons. The extended family also plays a role in the labor market, where social connections are vitally important in landing a job or career.

THE IMPACT OF RELIGION

Religion plays a much more important role in the lives of Mauritians than it does for most people in the West. The population is deeply religious for both personal and social reasons, and the different religious groups share a common stance in relation to permissiveness and lax morals.

Religion in Mauritius works on two levels: first, as devotional practice performed by different faiths and denominations (mainly Hinduism, Christianity, and Islam), and second, as a way of marking group identity in a multicultural society. Despite this religious communalism, the mixing of different traditions is common among islanders, who participate in each other's festivals and often worship at each other's shrines. Priests, pandits (Hindu scholars), and imams play an important role in Mauritian society, educating young people and offering leadership in community development work.

Religious beliefs influence the principles and practices of the different groups: Hindus generally promote sacrifice and thrift, Muslims are focused on promoting Islamic values in their communities, and many Creoles treat prayer and church attendance seriously. Mutual support and "helping one's own" are common within each religious community. What Westerners may think of as nepotism is not necessarily regarded as immoral by Mauritians: they may instead feel that they are acting religiously by helping their family and members of their own community.

RACISM AND COMMUNALISM

To a great extent, Mauritians are defined by their ethno-religious background and, within this, their class and/or caste. Identity is related to community and to the competition between the various groups for the country's resources and labor market, and a foreigner is likely to come across a surprising amount of racial intolerance on the island. This is in stark contrast to the commonly held view that Mauritians coexist in harmony. Referring to interethnic tension on the island, Mauritian writer Malcolm de Chazal once remarked that "this country cultivates sugarcane and prejudice."

A darker side of the Mauritian character can emerge if people feel that their culture or values are being threatened; there has been rioting along communal lines on several occasions. Such outbreaks of violence are rare, however, and racial tension in Mauritius is much more likely to be characterized by a simmering lack of trust between particularly intolerant members of each community. A whole range of pejorative names exists for the different ethnic groups, many of which hark back to slavery and the early years of the French colony. "Malbar" is a general term for Hindus, "Laskar" for Muslims, and Afro-Mauritians are sometimes referred to as "Mazambik" or "Nasion." There are widespread reports of racial discrimination toward Afro-Mauritians and Chagossians by the Mauritian authorities.

Whiteness and a lighter skin color is, regrettably, still seen as a sign of higher social status in Mauritius. Largely a legacy of the racial power structure of colonial society, exclusion still exists in the whites-only clubs of the Franco-Mauritian elite. David Vine writes about this racial hierarchy, or pigmentocracy: "Since the nineteenth century, people of French and British descent have remained at the top of the social, political, and economic hierarchies; people of mixed and Indian ancestry have occupied a middle stratum; Afro-Mauritian Creoles have remained primarily working class, generally at the bottom . . ."

Despite these interethnic issues, younger, educated Mauritians are hostile to this racialized worldview and have a more respectful attitude toward fellow Mauritians of different backgrounds. For them, Mauritian identity comes first and ethno-religious identity second.

THE GENDER DIVIDE

In their social lives outside the family, Mauritians usually associate only with members of the same sex. Although younger people have less traditional lifestyles and might mix more regularly with the opposite sex, this is often kept secret from their parents—it could lead to tensions in traditional families, who wish to protect their daughters from the advances of men. Arranged marriages, especially in the Hindu and Muslim communities, mean that many women are expected to move to a new town or village to live with a husband, close to his family. Women are generally expected to play a more submissive role than men, and family gatherings and other social occasions are often marked by segregation of the sexes—women prepare the food in the kitchen, while men prepare drinks and socialize in the lounge.

The position of Mauritian women is starting to change as greater employment opportunities and social mobility combine to break up the patriarchal order. Today they have the opportunity to become as educated as men. Sexist attitudes are still common, however, and access to senior positions in the workplace remains a challenge. It is normal for many young women to work (female employment has increased greatly in textiles and other manufacturing industries), although their mothers and grandmothers still play the traditional role of the housewife.

The implementation of laws against gender discrimination and domestic violence has helped to improve the life chances of Mauritian women, and feminist movements and women's organizations such as the Mauritius Alliance of Women have been instrumental in improving their situation.

CLOSENESS, GOSSIP, AND RUMORS
One aspect of life on a small island is the propensity of people to gossip and even be prone to hysteria. The degrees of separation between most Mauritians are so few that one Mauritian is likely to have at least heard of another's family name or know of them via a friend or relative. In this way, people are able to "place" each other socially and geographically with relative ease. In fact, many Mauritians like making local claims to fame by virtue of their closeness to people who have made their mark in society, such as politicians and other public figures (although here this is not seen to be as remarkable as it would be in the West). As a result of this proximity, sometimes accurate, often false, and frequently defamatory claims spread quickly through the country. This is aided in part by the local press, which thrives on gossip and rumor. Many foreigners and locals alike find this aspect of Mauritian culture stifling and unpleasant.

There is a long tradition of rumormongering on the island, with many Franco-Mauritian plantation owners defending their reputations in high-profile court cases in the eighteenth and nineteenth centuries. As a foreigner, instead of protesting your innocence or trying to refute unfounded rumors, it is much wiser for you to accept this phenomenon as an inevitable part of island life.

Fear of the Dark

One well-known rumor spread across the island during power outages following Cyclone Hollanda in 1994. Touni Minwi ("Naked at Midnight"), a kind of half-man, half-dog werewolf figure, was said to be walking the streets of Mauritius at night, preying on young women, whom he would rape. The hysteria spread like wildfire across the island and resulted in pronouncements from religious leaders and the formation of vigilante groups to find and attack the mythical beast.

ATTITUDES TO TIME

Mauritians are generally more relaxed about time than Westerners, especially in rural areas and on the island of Rodrigues. They are not likely to rush around to get things done, preferring a more leisurely approach to life, and are known to be poor timekeepers. If you are arranging a meeting, be aware that locals often arrive anywhere between fifteen minutes and half an hour late. The excuse that they are following "Mauritian time" suggests that it is normal and sometimes acceptable to be late, though the influence of global business culture may soon bring all this to an end. Either way, it is still important for foreigners to be punctual, especially in the business context.

Aside from their lack of punctuality, Mauritians generally follow an early-to-bed, early-to-rise regime.

WORK ETHIC

Although they do not work long hours (many finish by 4:00 p.m.) and might seem unhurried to outsiders, Mauritians are keen to work as long as it does not interfere with their private lives. Employees are unlikely to work longer than they have to, and definitely resent having to work evenings and weekends to meet deadlines. In rural areas, attitudes toward work are even more relaxed and carefree.

Nevertheless, there is a growing acceptance that a change in attitude is necessary if the country is to succeed in a globalized world, and the government is encouraging people to be more flexible with regard to working hours. A recent initiative has promoted the idea of Mauritius becoming a "24/7 economy," providing round-the-clock service to foreign clients.

chapter three

BELIEFS, TRADITIONS, & CELEBRATIONS

The traditions and festivals of Mauritius have their roots in Africa, Asia, and Europe, and an increasing number have actually developed on the island itself (such as Maha Shivaratree, the Père Laval pilgrimage, and the remembrance of slavery and indenture). Visitors are generally welcome to participate in them—indeed, most Mauritians encourage others to join them in celebrating their "unity in diversity."

RELIGION IN MAURITIUS

The Constitution guarantees freedom of belief, and the island is home to the world's three largest religions: Christianity, Islam, and Hinduism. Other religions, such as Buddhism and Sikhism, are practiced by small minorities. The importance of faith in Mauritian life is evident in the many festivals and in the large number of churches, mosques, temples, and shrines on the island.

When visiting religious sites, you should respect the local customs. Remove your shoes and any Western headwear when entering mosques and Hindu temples, dress modestly in all places of worship, and be respectful of worshippers if you are taking photographs. If in doubt, ask.

Hinduism

With around half the population professing to be Hindu, Hinduism is by far the dominant religion in Mauritius. Often known as *Sanatana Dharma* (the Eternal Way), it is a hugely complex and heterogeneous belief system and way of life with roots in the Indian subcontinent. Although far from uniform as a religion, at the heart of Hinduism is the belief in *dharma* (law or duty) and the dutiful ordering of one's life in order to attain reincarnation or release. Underpinning this is the belief in a soul or inner self (*atman*), in Brahman (God, or the Supreme Spirit), who is the underlying source of spiritual and physical existence, and in the natural moral law of *karma*, whereby an individual's past actions have either positive or negative consequences on their future. Meditation, the recitation of mantras, and the offering of gifts are central to the ritual worship of images or statues (*murtis*) of numerous deities, who often have animals as their "vehicles." Hindus respect animal life, and cows are considered sacred; followers do not eat beef, and many are vegetarians who avoid using any animal products.

The *Vedas* are the original sacred texts of Hinduism, written in Sanskrit. These form the basis of the rituals performed by orthodox Hindus at their temples (*mandirs*, or sometimes *kovils* or *shivalas*). Temples were first built in Mauritius in the mid-nineteenth century after the arrival of huge numbers of Indian indentured laborers. The sacred treatises of

the *Upanishads* are the source of Hindu
philosophy. Core beliefs and traditions are also
embodied in texts such as the *Puranas*, and the epic
poems of the *Mahabharata* and the *Ramayana*.

Hinduism places stress on purification (with
water) and sacrifice. Pilgrimage, festivals, and the
importance of rivers, lakes, and sacred places play
a significant role in the lives of Hindus. Offerings
of light, water, fruit, or incense are often made at
shrines in Hindu homes. Some aspects of
Hinduism—such as the class-based division of
labor (*varna*), the complex, hereditary caste
system (*jati*), and the importance of bodies of
water (especially the sea and, in the case of
Mauritius, the sacred crater lake, Ganga Talao)—
have been transferred to Mauritian society.

Due to its inherent lack of centralization,
Hinduism in Mauritius is organized along a
number of sectarian lines based on tradition and
the particular deity being worshipped. Sanatanists
form the orthodox majority, whereas the Arya
Samaj reform movement—which initially rejected
idolatry, the caste system, and influences external
to the religion—has gained supporters since the

late nineteenth century. There are also Marathi, Telugu, and Tamil variants of Hinduism, whose rituals and traditions have been preserved and whose temples are found across the island (the first large Tamil temple was built in Terre Rouge in 1843). A popular Tamil saying states, "*Koyil illa uril kudi irukka vendaam*" ("Do not live in a place where there is no temple"), and colorful temples across the island bear testament to this.

Mauritian Hindus of both north and south Indian origins have cultivated ties with Hindu organizations in India. The importance of the religious homeland is also evident in the fact that many Mauritian Hindus undertake pilgrimages to religious sites in India, and Indian missionaries have often visited and stayed on the island. Additionally, in the latter years of the twentieth century, religious and cultural organizations were set up to promote the interests of these specific groups, often receiving government grants and subsidies (the Mauritius Tamil Temples Federation was established in 1960, for example). The Hindu Council of Mauritius was formed in the 1970s in an attempt to unite all types of Hinduism on the island.

Hindu *baithkas* (community centers and youth clubs), where followers can develop their faith and learn Hindi, are found across Mauritius. Pandits and temple priests (*pujari*) command respect and power among members of their own community.

Christianity
Most Creoles and Franco-Mauritians, many Sino-Mauritians, and some Indo-Mauritians are

practicing Roman Catholics. Catholicism is the country's second-largest religion, practiced by almost a quarter of the population.

Catholicism, of course, rests on belief in the life and teachings of Jesus Christ, son of God, who was born human, was crucified in adulthood, and was resurrected to save humanity from sin and mortality. Catholics are expected to live a life of love and service in His name. They follow the

teachings of the Bible and participate in communion with God, Jesus Christ, and fellow Catholics through the Eucharist during Mass. Prayer and the sacraments of baptism, confirmation, and reconciliation (confession) are central to the religious life of Mauritian Catholics.

Roman Catholicism in Mauritius has historically been dominated by the Franco-Mauritians, and Catholic practices here are very European. The Church is administered by the Diocese of Port Louis and the Vicariate Apostolic of Rodrigues, led by the Archbishop of the Mascarenes and the Seychelles. The most important churches are the Saint Louis Cathedral in Port Louis and Saint Gabriel Cathedral in Rodrigues. Church attendance on Sunday is strong among Catholics, who also pay regular visits for private prayer. Mass is commonly held in French, and occasionally in Kreol.

Other Christian denominations such as Anglicanism are also present, but they have never been more than marginal due to the historical resistance of Indo-Mauritians to conversion and the strong opposition of the Franco-Mauritian elite to any Anglicization of the island.

Islam

Muslims make up around 17 percent of the Mauritian population, with the majority belonging to the orthodox Sunni Hanafi denomination or its subsects. Other denominations include a Shi'a minority and smaller numbers belonging to the Ahmadi sect.

Islam is centered on the belief in Allah (God), whose teachings were revealed through the Prophet Muhammad and articulated in the *Qur'an*, and in examples taken from Muhammad's life (the *Sunnah*). The faithful follow the five pillars of Islam: profession of faith in one God, Allah, with Muhammad as his messenger; prayers, at five points in the course of the day; fasting, during the holy month of Ramadan and also at other times; almsgiving; and the *hajj*, pilgrimage to Mecca at least once in one's lifetime. Alcohol and pork are  forbidden (*haram*) to observant Muslims.

Muslims worship at a number of mosques on the island, the most important by far being the Jummah Mosque in Port Louis, established in 1852.

The first mosque was permitted in 1805 at Camp des Lascars in Port Louis, and others were eventually built in the central plateau towns and smaller settlements in northern Mauritius. *Madrassas*, Islamic schools and youth clubs, can be found in areas where there is a strong Muslim presence. Urdu and Arabic are used in religious practice among Mauritian Muslims, although these languages are largely absent from everyday life. Kreol is increasingly used by preachers.

The partition of India in 1947 created a Hindu–Muslim division in Mauritian society. Today, however, most Mauritian Muslims look to the wider Islamic world, rather than to Pakistan, for cultural reference.

Buddhism, Taoism, and Confucianism
A very small number of Sino-Mauritians follow Buddhism, Taoism, or the teachings of Confucius. Chinese pagodas in Port Louis and other settlements are important sites for traditional ceremonies and festivals.

SHRINES AND PILGRIMAGES
Shrines are very important sites in Mauritius, as befits a religious nation.

Père Laval
The shrine to nineteenth-century French missionary priest Père Laval at Sainte-Croix, in the suburbs of Port Louis, attracts hundreds of thousands of devotees each year on the anniversary of his death. Catholics and Mauritians of other

faiths travel from across the island and around the world, sometimes carrying crosses and praying on their way to his tomb. On September 8 and 9, a vigil is held and offerings are placed at the site of his effigy. Also at other times of year, huge numbers of devotees travel to the shrine to lay wreaths, place candles, and pray for protection and good health.

From 1841, Père Jacques-Désiré Laval spent more than twenty years of his life in Mauritius among poor, sick, uneducated former slaves, improving their conditions and introducing them to the Catholic faith. He was beatified by Pope John Paul II on April 24, 1979, and a small museum at the church explains the life and religious acts of the "Apostle of the Blacks."

Ganga Talao

Ganga Talao—Lake of the Ganges, or Grand Bassin to non-Hindus—is a consecrated site where one finds temples and numerous shrines to Hindu deities. A small amount of water from the sacred Ganges River was transferred into Grand Bassin in the 1970s, thereby fulfilling a local myth that this crater lake was formed by the deity Shiva dropping water from the great river onto Mauritius. Here, Mangal Mahadev, a 108-foot (33-meter) statue of Shiva unveiled in 2007, is the tallest statue on the island. Since 1898, Ganga Talao has been the end point of a major pilgrimage during the annual Maha Shivaratree festival (see page 73).

Jummah Mosque

Muslims often visit the tombs of spiritual teachers from India and Mauritius at the Jummah Mosque in Port Louis. Here, devotees make vows and perform offerings.

BIRTHS, NAMING CEREMONIES, AND BIRTHDAYS

Births are a happy time for all families, who naturally celebrate according to their own traditions. Among Hindus, a naming ceremony is held nine days after the birth of the child, following which its head may be shaven. Muslims hold a family feast (during which sheep are sacrificed) and hold a naming ceremony within a week of the birth, while Creoles are likely to have a Catholic baptism and family celebration for the child. Sino-

Mauritians hold a naming ceremony approximately one month after a child is born.

Mauritian given names generally reflect the ancestral culture. Creoles, many Sino-Mauritians, and some Indo-Mauritians have French or English names (such as Marie, Patrice, or Michael), often including a number of middle names. Spanish and Italian names (Sylvio and Giovanni, for example) are also fashionable for boys, despite the negligible influence of these countries on Mauritian history. Muslims often have traditional Islamic or Arabic names (such as Ameera or Nadeem), and Hindus follow their own traditions (Priya or Ashvin, for example). It is not uncommon for Mauritians to use an "official" given name when dealing with the authorities, and another name at home with family and close friends—either a nickname, a middle name, or another name altogether.

Birthdays are important events, especially for children. Extended families gather together to offer gifts and food, and to listen to music and take numerous photographs. Westernized birthday parties involving candles and balloons are common.

WEDDINGS

Weddings are often celebrated on a large scale in Mauritius, with close friends and extended family arriving from around the world. Guests are also invited from across the communal divide. It is an opportunity to eat, dance, and, in some cases, drink to excess. Don't be surprised if you see a cameraman following the bride and groom from dawn to dusk. Wedding videos are big business.

Honeymoons often involve staying in a luxury hotel or a rented seaside bungalow in Mauritius, or if the couple is wealthy, a trip abroad to South Africa or another country in the Indian Ocean. Wedding gifts depend on the background of the giver, but they normally consist of money or items for the couple's new home.

Many Mauritians also have a low-key civil wedding, which will take place before the religious ceremony. Although religious weddings are sufficient in the eyes of the law, this practice persists among the population.

If you'd like to tie the knot in Mauritius, check that the wedding satisfies the law in your own country. Of course, many companies and tour operators already cater to this market.

The Hindu Wedding

Hindu weddings vary according to the couple's background, but traditionally take place over the course of a few days. A reception (the *gamat*, actually two receptions—one for the bride, one for the groom) is held in a temporary tent in a garden or yard the night before the ceremony, and involves traditional Indian food, the exchanging of gifts and the dowry, and some music and dancing. Turmeric paste is often rubbed into the hands and faces of the couple as a sign of purification. The ceremony itself usually takes place at the local temple, with the bride resplendent in a traditional red sari and gold jewelry, and the groom wearing either a modern suit or traditional garb and a turban. Couples perform various rituals in the company of the priest, such as placing a sacred yellow cord (the *thali*) around the bride's neck and presenting themselves in front of a sacred fire, which they then walk around seven times.

The Muslim Wedding

A Muslim wedding ceremony (the *nikah*) usually takes place at the mosque, accompanied by prayers in Urdu or Arabic. The ceremony entails the signing of the marriage contract by the bride and groom. Following this, guests are invited to a reception meal (the *walima*).

Bride and groom often wear Western-style wedding outfits, namely a white dress and veil for the woman and a suit for the man. More traditional weddings involve a wedding gown, a white garland, and jewels for the bride. It is usual for the bride's hands and feet to be ornately painted with henna. At both the mosque and the wedding meal, men and women sit separately. Alcohol is obviously absent, and guests are served soft drinks or water. At the end of the ceremony, a pastry called a *soutal finn* is offered to guests.

Celebrations usually take place in a rented reception hall or sometimes just a tent. They are accompanied by music, cake, soft drinks, and the exchanging of gifts between families, sometimes in the form of money stuffed in envelopes.

Creole and Christian Weddings

Creoles have a reputation as the island's party animals, and their weddings are known for their extravagance, sometimes preceded by Western practices such as bachelor and bachelorette parties (*l'enterrement de vie de garcon/ de jeune fille*). Following a church ceremony involving the exchanging of rings and marriage vows in the mid-afternoon on a Friday or Saturday, wedding photographs are taken and a reception is often held at a hall, restaurant, or hotel. This involves speeches, sega and pop music, fireworks, copious amounts of food and alcohol, and a beautiful wedding cake. After leaving the reception, guests often continue to celebrate at home throughout the night. Brides normally wear traditional white wedding dresses, and grooms often dress in an expensive suit.

Chinese Weddings

Many Sino-Mauritians have Catholic weddings, but traditional Confucian or Buddhist weddings involve the respective families exchanging gifts and a dowry, conducting processions between each other's houses, and performing prayers at family altars. Newlyweds are taken to a bridal suite and undertake a tea ceremony.

FUNERALS

Mauritians accept death as part and parcel of life, and belief in the afterlife is widespread. Hindus and Buddhists believe in reincarnation and rebirth, whereas Christians and Muslims believe in different versions of the concept of heaven and hell.

Influential public figures are often given state funerals, and days of mourning are declared for the population. The funeral of "Father of the Nation" Sir Seewoosagur Ramgoolam, in 1985, drew hundreds of thousands onto the streets, and many more watched on television at home. For ordinary folk, funeral rites generally follow the practices of one of the island's various religions. A death is often followed by a wake at the home of the deceased's family, and the funeral takes place within a day or two. It is common among Christians to place flowers at the grave of a relative, especially around the time of religious festivals.

Catholic funerals, involving prayers, hymns, and a burial, usually take place at a local parish church, . A minority of Christians cremate their loved ones. Sino-Mauritians (mostly Catholics and Buddhists) hold an additional annual memorial for all dead relatives each April. Muslim burials take place within twenty-four hours of death and are followed by three days of mourning.

Hindus cremate their dead. They often bear the body on a stretcher decorated with flowers (a *tatri*) in a procession to the crematorium. Mauritian Hindus sometimes abstain from festivals and celebrations for up to a year after a relative's death, and ceremonies are usually held annually to commemorate the passing of a loved one.

HOLIDAYS AND FESTIVALS

The Mauritian calendar reflects and respects the diverse nature of the population. Mauritians will often participate in the festivals of other ethnic and religious groups, which means that there is a lot of celebrating at all times of year. Islanders often combine public holidays with generous extra days off work in order to take a long weekend (known as a *pon* or *pont*, meaning a bridge). Some public holidays are fixed, whereas others follow non-Western calendars and vary each year.

PUBLIC HOLIDAYS

Fixed Dates

January 1 and 2	New Year (sometimes also a weekday added onto a weekend)
February 1	Abolition of Slavery
March 12	National Day (Independence Day)
May 1	Labor Day
November 1	All Saints' Day
November 2	Arrival of Indentured Laborers
December 25	Christmas

Moveable Dates

January/February	Thaipoosam Cavadee
January/February	Chinese Spring Festival (Chinese New Year)
February/March	Maha Shivaratree
March/April	Ougadi (Telegu New Year)
September	Ganesh Chaturthi
October/November	Divali
Varies	Eid ul-Fitr (end of Ramadan)

Festivals

New Year's Eve

New Year's Eve in Mauritius is celebrated by members of all communities and usually involves fireworks being set off in front yards and gardens around the island.

National Day

National Day (also Independence Day or Republic Day), on March 12, sees members of all communities gathering at the Champ de Mars racecourse for a state-sponsored multicultural festival of music, dance, and speeches televised for the nation. National flags are everywhere and it is common for members of the National Assembly to visit schools across the island to deliver the prime minister's annual message, followed by cakes, soft drinks, and performances by pupils.

Maha Shivaratree

Hindus in Mauritius celebrate a number of festivals, including Maha Shivaratree ("The Great Night of Shiva"), a pilgrimage usually undertaken in February in honor of the deity Shiva. Devotees dressed in white carry a wooden arch adorned with flowers (the *kanwar*) and other items to the sacred lake of Ganga Talao in southern Mauritius. Here, they pray, offer food, flowers, and statues to deities, and collect holy water, which they pour over effigies of Shiva and use to purify themselves. Many devotees undergo a fast in the weeks prior to the pilgrimage, which involves up to 500,000 devotees and can take several days, including vigils. This is the largest Hindu festival outside India.

Holi

Holi, the Hindu festival of color celebrating the triumph of good over evil, takes place in February or March. It involves people throwing brightly colored water, paint, and powder over each other in a celebration marking the beginning of spring, and is preceded by the communal burning of a large bonfire (the *holika dahan*).

Divali

Divali, or the five-day "Festival of Light" in October
or November, sees
Hindus lighting
lamps inside and
outside their homes
to celebrate the
inner light that
shines through the
darkness of
ignorance and fear.

Ougadi

Hindus of south and west Indian ancestry also have
their own festivals. Ougadi, the Telegu New Year, is
usually celebrated in March.

Thaipoosam Cavadee and Tamil Festivals

Tamils celebrate Thaipoosam Cavadee for ten days
in January or February in honor of the deity
Muruga, symbolizing the struggle against ignorance
and evil. Devotees undertake a pilgrimage and
perform a rite involving the piercing of the body
with needles, skewers, and hooks. A wooden arch
adorned with flowers and pots of milk (the *cavadee*)
is carried by pilgrims in a state of trance to their
deity at the temple. Other Tamil festivals include
Varusha Pirappu (New Year), Govinden (fasting in
September/October), and Teemeedee (fire-walking
to symbolize self-sacrifice over evil).

Ganesh Chathurti

Ganesh Chathurti, which takes place in September,
is the birthday of Ganesha, the Hindu god of

wisdom and remover of obstacles. It is celebrated by Hindus of Marathi origin.

Ramadan, Eid ul-Fitr, and Other Muslim Festivals
Muslims observe a fast during daylight hours in the holy month of Ramadan, which ends with the feast of Eid ul-Fitr.

Eid ul-Adha marks the end of the annual *hajj*, the pilgrimage to Mecca that is required of all Muslims at some point in their lives. This is often followed by prayers and the sacrificing of a goat or sheep.

Yamsey commemorates the martyrdom of Hussein, grandson of the Prophet Muhammad; it involves large processions where devotees carry *ghoons* (towers representing martyrs' tombs), chant, beat drums, and shake tambourines in the Plaine Verte area of Port Louis. This festival is held by Shi'a Muslims during the holy month of Muharram.

Yom an-Nabi commemorates the birth of the Prophet. The Islamic calendar is lunar, and the date may vary in relation to the Gregorian calendar.

Christian Festivals
Mauritian Christians celebrate Christmas, Easter, the Assumption of the Blessed Virgin Mary, and many other festivals. Many also undertake the Père Laval Pilgrimage on September 8 and 9, where pilgrims travel to the shrine of Père Jacques-Désiré Laval to pray for healing and good health.

International Creole Day
Many Creoles (and other Mauritians) celebrate International Creole Day on October 28, in common with Creoles in other countries.

Chinese Spring Festival (New Year)
Chinese Spring Festival (New Year), in January, sees a profusion of red around Chinatown in Port Louis, and firecrackers are set off to deter evil spirits. Sino-Mauritians gather together huge quantities of food to symbolize bounty for the coming year, and "wax cakes" (made of flour and honey) are offered to friends and relatives.

REMEMBERING SLAVERY AND INDENTURE

Remembering the struggles of one's ancestors is important to the majority of the population. As a country, Mauritius is still coming to terms with its joint history of slavery and mass immigration of predominantly South Asian indentured laborers. The histories of these two institutions have often been regarded as separate, but the population is increasingly seeing the two as linked, and a combined effort to place both at the heart of Mauritian history and memory will certainly play a role in forging a shared identity in years to come.

Slavery

Slavery existed in Mauritius from the first Dutch settlement in the sixteenth century until its abolition in 1835, and its repercussions are still felt by Afro-Mauritian Creoles, who suffer racial discrimination and exclusion as part of their daily lives. Public remembrance of this history has only recently become more visible. Each year, on February 1, Mauritians commemorate the abolition of slavery by laying wreaths at a monument to slaves in Mahébourg. Another monument exists in the Company Gardens in Port Louis, and the "Monument to an Unknown Slave" was erected outside the Port Louis Theatre in 1998.

In 2008, Le Morne Brabant, a rugged, mountainous peninsula where maroons (fugitive slaves) set up free communities beyond the reach of the slave owners in the nineteenth century, became a potent symbol of resistance to slavery when it was listed as a UNESCO World Heritage Site. Legend has it that when British soldiers arrived to announce the abolition of slavery, maroons living on Le Morne thought the party had been sent to capture them. Tragically, out of defiance, many are said to have jumped hundreds of feet to their deaths.

A monument was unveiled at the base of Le Morne in 2009, with a plaque displaying words by Mauritian poet Sedley Richard Assonne:

> "There were hundreds of them, but my people
>   the maroons
> chose the kiss of death over the chains of slavery.
> Never must we forget their noble deed
> Written in the pages of history for the sake
> of humanity . . ."

The Indenture System

The institution of indenture began in November 1834 and was abolished in May 1924. In ninety years, as many as half a million Indians, and some Chinese and other nationalities, were brought to Mauritius to work in the island's sugarcane fields, work which had previously been done by slaves.

The Aapravasi Ghat (Immigration Depot) is the building in the harbor of Port Louis where these immigrants were processed upon their arrival in Mauritius. The site has been listed as a UNESCO World Heritage Site since 2006. Each year, on November 2, Mauritians commemorate the sacrifices of the indentured laborers by laying wreaths on the historic steps of Aapravasi Ghat.

FOLKLORE AND SUPERSTITIONS

Many Mauritians, especially in rural areas, believe in witchcraft and the paranormal, in what is probably a fusion of African, Malagasy, Indian, Chinese, and European folk traditions.

Lougarou (a werewolf or wolf man) is a notorious figure in Mauritian folklore. He apparently appears at a full moon and wreaks havoc among the population. The figure is likely to be a combination of French and African folklore, and is mostly used to scare children. Protection can be offered by consulting a local sorcerer or witch doctor (*longanis* or *treter*).

Witch doctors are often called upon to cure infertility, sexual ailments (with love potions), and sickness, to bring good luck in one's professional life, or to read one's future (using lentils, pebbles, or grains of rice). Others treat the possessed, and perform rituals to bring harm to the patient's enemies. The *longanis* normally chants, uses plants, spices, and other local ingredients, and sometimes sacrifices a cat or a cockerel as part of the ritual, which is often performed in cemeteries or in places where people have died, such as traffic blackspots at crossroads and junctions, where the requisite supernatural energy is said to be high.

Skeptics—and there are many in the various religious communities—see practitioners as simply profiting from others' misfortunes, or as charlatans making huge sums from people's fears. Although it is marginal and somewhat secretive, there are enough practitioners and enough money in the trade for it to have become a national concern. Mauritian law takes a dim view of the practice of black magic, which can land a practitioner with a short prison sentence and a fine.

As in many other countries, superstitions abound in Mauritius, especially among the older generation. These will vary from family to family and between communities, but failure to heed them is believed to result in bad luck, death, or *movezer* (*mauvais air*, or evil spirits). Some of the more peculiar superstitions include:

- Don't stand under a tree after 6:00 p.m., and definitely do not pick fruit or leaves at this time.
- If returning home after dark, you should enter the house backward to make sure evil spirits do not enter with you.
- Don't sweep the floor after 6:00 p.m.
- Don't leave your clothes outside after dark.
- Don't cut your nails on a Friday, and never cut them indoors.
- If many dogs are howling on the streets, it is a warning that someone is about to die.
- Avoid using knives and scissors at Chinese New Year.
- Don't take photos of three people together.

chapter four

MAKING FRIENDS

Mauritians are very warm, friendly, and helpful, especially with foreigners, and this quality is put to good use in the tourist industry and when doing business with international clients. Due to their multicultural history, most Mauritians are also open to different cultures and accepting of foreigners' different customs and ways, even if these appear eccentric and sometimes immoral to them. Do not assume that the locals will crowd round you to shake your hand or ruffle your hair just because you are a foreigner; as we've noted, Mauritians are actually more reserved than you might expect and will give strangers plenty of space when they first meet them.

FRIENDSHIP BETWEEN MAURITIANS

Once you've got over the initial impression of Mauritians as a warm and hospitable people, you will realize that real friendship in Mauritius takes some time and a great deal of effort to nurture.

A good friend—known locally as a *kamarad*—is not a fleeting acquaintance or business contact (or possibly someone using your high status as a foreigner to earn them a favor), but a person with whom you have shared good times and bad and built a solid foundation of trust and mutual respect. Traditionally, great emphasis has been placed on two individuals introducing each other to their families and being made to feel completely welcome by them. Today, however, social networks are increasingly being formed on the basis of other bonds, such as work, sports (watching and participating), and random encounters. Many Mauritian men also have drinking partners, who they do not necessarily know outside the environment of the bar.

Friends will often spend weekends, bank holidays, and many evenings with each other, frequently dropping in unannounced. Friendship in Mauritius might involve sharing in a number of activities, most notably meals and drinks, trips to the beach, boat trips, hiking in the mountains and forests, gambling, shopping for clothes, and trips to the cinema. Mauritian friends of all ethnic groups are usually quite welcome at each other's weddings and festivals, and foreigners who have developed a friendship with a Mauritian are more than likely to be invited to join in any of these activities.

MEETING PEOPLE

When socializing in Mauritius, it is vital to have a good understanding of the social hierarchies and interethnic relations on the island. Communal and ethnic groups tend to be exclusive, and there is also an implicit ethnic hierarchy, which means that foreigners who are white tend to be given greater respect just because of the color of their skin.

As a foreigner, your attitude to Mauritian customs and culture will go a long way toward securing a lasting friendship. Although many islanders will be more than capable of conversing with you in English, even a little knowledge of French and/or Kreol will demonstrate that you are willing to speak to them on their own terms. Although they live on a small island seemingly stranded in a vast ocean, a condescending attitude will not go over well. It would be wiser and more productive to try to understand the complex, cosmopolitan nature of the country and not to write Mauritians off as ignorant of the outside world; they are actually very familiar with the Western media and ways of life.

Although it is common for a Mauritian's family and friends to drop in unannounced, a degree of tact should be employed when deciding to visit a Mauritian at home. If you haven't been invited to dinner, it would obviously be impolite to visit friends when they are likely to be eating.

If you are a new expat arriving in Mauritius, a useful Web site to consult both before you leave and while you establish yourself on the island is Expat Mauritius (www.expatmauritius.com), which provides information and contacts for anyone looking for new friends on the island. Corona Worldwide has three branches on the island for befriending international women (www.coronaworldwide.org). The British Council in Rose Hill can be a useful place to meet friendly locals hoping to improve their English. Otherwise, local sports and leisure clubs are generally quite welcoming, as are social organizations such as the Rotary Club, which are found in the large towns and Port Louis. Local bars in residential areas can be rough-and-ready places in which to meet down-to-earth locals, but if you are looking for more sophisticated company, pubs, bars, and hotels in Port Louis (at the Caudan Waterfront complex) and the major tourist resorts such as Grand Baie and Flic en Flac are more appropriate.

TOPICS OF CONVERSATION AND TABOO SUBJECTS

Mauritians like to talk politics, and gossip and rumors are an essential part of island life. If you have a good understanding of local politics, you might want to comment on recent elections and political debates; be careful not to take this too far, though, since Mauritian politics is often ethnically aligned and your friends and acquaintances will have deeply entrenched views about their political representatives. When talking about international affairs, do not assume that Mauritians are isolated in their own little bubble in the Indian Ocean. Their access to the international media means they are in touch with the outside world.

Another risky subject is money, which often causes embarrassment when brought up in conversation. Many Mauritians like to present themselves as well-off, even if they have to struggle each month to make ends meet.

Although it is recommended that you learn about the different ethnic and religious groups in

Mauritius—which will, of course, give you a better understanding of what you are experiencing and make your stay more enriching—it would be wise not to get too involved in discussions on this subject. When it comes to ethnicity, culture, and religion, the Mauritian way is to respect the country's diversity—in public at least. Although members of the different ethnic groups often talk about each other disparagingly in private, this is rarely something that will be aired publicly in a mixed group of Mauritians. In fact, talking "race" is one of the main taboos on the island. Many Mauritians are reluctant to talk about their mixed race, especially if family reputation is at stake.

Conversely, Mauritians are often happy to talk about the eventful history of their country, but take care not to push people too far on touchy subjects such as slavery, injustice, and exploitation. The effects of French and British colonial rule are still felt by marginalized groups of poor Creoles and Indo-Mauritians, and the Chagos islanders who were forcibly removed from their homes on Diego Garcia.

On a lighter note, safe topics of conversation revolve around soccer (many Mauritian men are crazy about British football), music (Mauritian, Indian, and Western), popular culture, and entertainment. Mauritians will also be very keen to learn about your own customs and traditions.

Finally, sex is seldom talked about in public, and is least appropriate as a topic of conversation in the company of conservative members of the various religious communities. Any mention of sex is likely to be restricted to groups of men hoping to impress their peers and you, if you're a male foreigner.

If you do make a faux pas by breaking a taboo, you are unlikely to be verbally or physically abused. Some Mauritians will give you the silent treatment, but others are more likely to be amused by your ignorance and lack of savoir faire.

INVITATIONS HOME

Mauritians are more likely to invite you home for a meal than they are to invite you out. If you are invited, you should make every effort to accept the offer—this is a great opportunity to meet a friend's family and to experience a healthy dose of Mauritian hospitality.

Etiquette will vary according to the host's background, but it would be polite at least to offer to remove your shoes before entering the house. In terms of dress, smart-casual clothing is normally appropriate; in general, you should avoid wearing anything that could offend people's sensibilities (no beachwear or short skirts, for example). If you want to bring a gift, a bottle of good wine would be appropriate for a Francophile Mauritian; otherwise flowers, a cake, or cookies are fine when visiting someone who doesn't drink alcohol. Gifts are gratefully received, even if they aren't always expected.

If you are invited for supper, you will probably be asked to arrive slightly early in the evening to allow time for socializing. You will be shown into the lounge and offered a variety of *gajaks* (snacks) and alcoholic or nonalcoholic drinks depending on the host's culture. In such a situation, it is common for the guests to form distinct groups based on gender and generation: men and women talk separately, and children and adults socialize apart. The meal will consist of a hearty dish with guests sitting around a large table, or possibly a barbecue (*griyad* or *grillade*) on the patio or driveway outside.

If you are a close friend you can expect to stay well into the evening, when the mood is likely to become more relaxed as your hosts begin to wind down by watching television. However, bear in mind that the day starts early in many Mauritian households, especially during the week, and many families are not accustomed to staying up to socialize late into the night.

COURTSHIP AND DATING
Due to entrenched traditional views and the fact that news and rumor travel fast here, it is unusual for platonic friendships to develop between men and women. Many families are protective of their daughters, and you are much more likely to meet members of the opposite sex when in the company of a mixed group of family, friends, or colleagues.

The etiquette surrounding meeting partners and courting varies greatly according to ethno-religious community. Many Indo-Mauritians (both Hindu and Muslim) continue to practice arranged marriage, which is evidence of the important role played by the family in this society. Traditional Catholic and other Christian families might also be wary of their children's prospective partners, especially if there is a risk of breaking religious taboos such as premarital sex and the use of contraception. Some Mauritians are hostile toward mixed marriages and dating outside their own ethnic group. Nevertheless, people are becoming more liberal in their attitudes, and it is now much more common to see relationships developing between members of different communities. Internet dating is even a viable option for many young Mauritians.

If a couple decides to become more committed through engagement and marriage, it is normal for them to seek approval from their families, if only to maintain the importance of the family as an institution. Premarital sex is common, but it is a taboo that people rarely speak about.

If, as a foreigner in Mauritius, you decide to start a relationship with a Mauritian, you should be aware of these cultural and religious attitudes. The more respectful you are of a Mauritian's background, the more likely it is that you will be accepted as a respectable partner.

chapter five

THE MAURITIANS AT HOME

THE FAMILY

The extended family is central to the lives of most Mauritians. It is not only parents but also grandparents, aunts, and uncles who perform a key role in the upbringing of children, and this has increasingly been the case since Mauritian women began to be better integrated into the labor market. Nevertheless, with Westernization and social pressures coming into play, less and less emphasis is being placed on living in close proximity to one's extended family and this traditional support network is being eroded.

Following traditional norms, even working women are routinely expected to perform household duties and take care of the children. The traditional role of the man is that of breadwinner, although social changes mean that many men are also taking on domestic chores. Most Mauritians expect to care for their elderly relatives rather than deposit them in retirement homes; this is seen as an unquestionable duty. The retirement age is currently sixty-five, and life expectancy is approximately sixty-nine for men and seventy-six for women.

Although family planning initiatives mean that birthrates are declining, it is still common for families to have many children. In the mid-twentieth century it was usual for mothers to have between four and seven children, but now they are much more likely to have between two and four.

Marriage

Mauritians still overwhelmingly favor commitment to a life partner. A partner is someone who integrates well with your own family, is faithful, and provides support and often financial security.

Mauritians, as a rule, only marry within their own ethno-religious group, particularly the Hindu, Muslim, and Franco-Mauritian communities. Traditional Indo-Mauritians (both Hindus and Muslims), we have seen, also often have arranged marriages, where the bride will come to live with

the groom's family after the wedding. The matchmaking involves calling upon a large network of friends, colleagues, and relatives (sometimes overseas in India and the West) to find the right partner, after which an engagement party will be held. Creoles, being of mixed ancestry, tend to be more open and relaxed about the identity of marriage partners. Intermarriage between different ethno-religious communities is on the increase, especially in urban areas, although this still causes a stir among some traditionalists.

Often the choice of partner reflects the way in which the country is organized socially, with class, caste, religion, ethnicity, language, and education important factors that are taken into account, if only at a subconscious level. However, intermarriage can involve the conversion of one of the partners to the other's religion—Creoles to Islam, or Hindus and Sino-Mauritians to Catholicism, for example. If this is not tolerated by the families involved, say in marriages between Hindus or Franco-Mauritians and Muslims, the couple will have a very difficult time living in Mauritian society, founded as it is on family and ethno-religious identity.

Divorce is still rare, which is understandable considering the traditional religious background. Many feel a sense of shame if their children's marriages turn out to be unsuccessful.

Building a Home
Mauritians often wait until they are married before moving out of the family home. This is due to a combination of traditional values and financial

pressures. Poor and also more traditional families can still be found sharing a home between three generations. Moving out often involves building on top of the single-story family home or even building a new property on family-owned land, with the financial and practical assistance of family members. Rich families are often landowners who like the idea of dividing their land up between their children to use for future generations.

Children and Growing Up

The population is relatively young—around a quarter of Mauritians are under the age of fifteen. Children live quite a sheltered existence; the close and extended family is always there to offer guidance and to bring any wayward child into line. Officially children are not allowed to work until they reach the age of fifteen, but it is common for some to "help out" in family businesses. Although social problems such as drugs, alcohol  abuse, and child prostitution do exist, it is very rare to find Mauritian children and teenagers running afoul of the law. Gun and knife crimes are almost nonexistent among the young, except for the impoverished areas of Port Louis.

If you are a foreign visitor, Mauritians will be very warm and welcoming toward your children and will be more than happy for them to come with you when you visit their homes. They will encourage them to join their own children at mealtime and on days out.

EDUCATION

Education is a primary concern for Mauritians, who want their children to benefit more than they did from opportunities in the world of work. Many parents will sacrifice a great deal for their children. Bear in mind that a large number of elderly and middle-aged Mauritians have never completed even a secondary education.

Literacy on the island, according to the 2000 census, is approximately 85 percent (88.7 percent for men; 81.5 percent for women), making Mauritius one of the most literate, educated nations in the Africa region.

A system of free secondary education was implemented in 1976 and has been one of the driving forces behind the growth and diversification of the economy. Free and compulsory British-style education exists for children up to the age of sixteen. Instruction is normally in English, although some teachers often switch to French, Kreol, or Bhojpuri to explain the finer points to their pupils. A few state schools are coeducational; the majority restrict their intake to either boys or girls. A dozen or so schools are religious, especially Roman Catholic.

The school year runs from January to November, comprising three terms. School vacations take place at the end of April (two weeks), in July (three or four weeks), and in summer (usually from November until early January).

Primary Education

Many Mauritians to try to use personal contacts to secure places for their children at respected schools. From the ages of five to eleven, children are given a good grounding in general education and are encouraged to learn "ancestral" languages if they are from the Hindu, Tamil, Muslim, or Chinese communities. An exam, leading to the Certificate of Primary Education, is taken at ten or eleven, signaling entry into secondary school.

Secondary and Further Education

State secondary schooling is based on the English system, with the Cambridge Secondary School Certificate (after five years) and the Higher School Certificate (a further two years) being the benchmarks of academic success. The Royal Colleges at Port Louis and Curepipe are the most prestigious state establishments (both boys only), and are often the alma maters of leading statesmen. Vocational training is also available, and a number of private schools exist mainly for wealthier families. Families with the means often supplement secondary education with private tuition after school and on weekends. This can be a lucrative trade for teachers and lecturers who are sometimes poorly paid by the state system.

A handful of private schools—such as the prestigious Lycée La Bourdonnais in Curepipe—offer a highly respected French-style education.

University

In Mauritius, higher education is available at the University of Mauritius, the University of Technology, and a number of other establishments. A broad range of technical and academic courses are offered to an increasingly educated population. The Mahatma Gandhi Institute is a center of excellence for the study of Asian and African languages and cultures.

Scholarships and family assistance allow some Mauritians to move to Réunion, South Africa, India, France, or the UK for university education.

Adult Education

Many religious and left-wing organizations offer education to believers and workers respectively. One of the latter such organizations, Ledikasyon Pu Travayer, has been offering education to workers in the Kreol language since the 1970s.

Municipal libraries exist in Port Louis and some of the central plateau towns. The National Library in Port Louis houses thousands of books and documents relating to the country's social history, going back to the seventeenth century.

DAILY LIFE

Foreigners may take some time to adjust to the slower pace of life in Mauritius. Outside the main tourist areas and international businesses, daily life takes place between the hours of 9:00 a.m. and 4:30 p.m.—and Rodrigues is even more laid-back than its big sister Mauritius. Mauritians are not ones to stay out late at night, and are much more likely to go to bed early and rise early the next day.

A greater number of Mauritians now have access to stable employment. There has traditionally been a gender-defined division of labor. Women, if they work outside the home, mostly hold positions in sectors such as teaching, nursing, and the service industries. Since the 1970s, a much larger number of women has been employed in textiles and manufacturing. Men, on the other hand, have traditionally worked in transport, construction, engineering, technology, the public sector, and the import-export business. Both sexes work in tourism and hospitality. Work on Rodrigues is largely restricted to fishing, agriculture, and tourism. Overall unemployment in Mauritius, lower than it used to be, stood at around 7 percent in 2010. Monthly salaries are much lower than in North America and Europe, with wages as low as Rs4,000 for unskilled labor (around US$130 a month) rising to around Rs30,000 or more for work as a journalist (US$1,007 a month), but remember that the cost of living is proportionately lower too.

MEALS OF THE DAY

There is little time in the morning to eat breakfast together, so cereal, fruit, or a quick slice of bread with a topping (a *tartine*) is common. This might be accompanied by tea, coffee, or fruit juice.

Lunch is normally eaten at school or work, and is usually a small snack rather than a large meal. Workers might duck out to eat cheap, fast street food such as *dal pouri* (see page 105).

Supper is by far the most important meal of the day in terms of bringing the family together to talk about the day and to plan activities, and tends to be served in much larger quantities than breakfast or lunch. Some people follow the traditional practice of only eating with their right hand, but table manners are generally thoroughly Western.

It is quite common for Mauritians to eat snacks between meals. Predinner snacks called *gajak* are accompanied by alcoholic drinks; they might include chips, olives, pastries, cheese, slices of meat, or Indian-style pastries.

SHOPPING

Everyday shopping generally involves a trip to one of the many markets for cheap fish, meat, spices, and fresh fruit and vegetables. Daily items can also be bought from the local general store (*laboutik*), traditionally owned and run by a Sino-Mauritian family (many people still call their local shop the *laboutik sinwa*).

Large supermarkets often sell not just food and household goods but also clothes, toys, books, and newspapers. Prices tend to be lower in the central plateau towns, far from the main tourist areas.

Clothes are often bought at the market or at one of the modern shopping malls. Le Ruisseau Créole, located near Tamarin, is one of the most modern, high-end shopping centers. Malls at the Caudan

Waterfont (Port Louis), Orchard Centre (Quatre Bornes), and various towns in the central plateau also provide retail outlets selling clothes, books, CDs, and household items. If older Mauritians say they are going *an vil* (*en ville*, to town) to do their shopping, this usually means that they are heading into Port Louis.

PETS

Mauritians are not as attached to animals as Westerners are, and pets are not as popular on the island as in other parts of the world. It is common to see stray cats and dogs on residential streets, often fouling the public spaces (like in France, but without the sophisticated surroundings).

The most common pet in Mauritius is the dog, although its status is more that of a guard than man's best friend. Guard dogs are often kept outside in the yard or in a kennel, and you may be disturbed by their aggressive behavior as you walk past the gates of family homes. Mauritians tend to respond to this by using sticks, stones, and other missiles to scare them away.

DRESS AND CLOTHING

The majority of Mauritians wear Western-style clothes in day-to-day life, but fashion is influenced by the varied origins of the population. What people wear depends largely on vague rules related to formality, the urban–rural divide, ethno-religious identity, and simple personal preference.

Bright colors are worn by Mauritians of all backgrounds, especially the women. Creole dress, most typically the bright blouses and long skirts worn by sega dancers, often displays colorful patterns. Some traditional Indo-Mauritians wear the *dhoti kurta* (a long piece of cloth wrapped around a man's waist and legs, with a loose, collarless shirt on top), while others combine this with a Western-style shirt. The sari, other traditional clothing, and bright jewelry is usual among traditional Indo-Mauritian women,

especially in rural areas. Some Muslim women wear the head scarf, and a minority cover themselves completely with the *burqa*, while their male counterparts may wear cloth skullcaps or even a fez for significant religious events. Many devout Hindus, especially rural women, wear a *tika* (or *tilaka*, red dot) on the forehead and also paste henna into the parting of their hair. This is to show that they are married. Mauritians of all walks of life wear sandals or flip-flops (known locally as *savat*), perfectly suited to the climate.

Visitors should be aware that although beachwear and tight or revealing clothing may be acceptable in many resorts, they are not appropriate in towns and villages away from the tourist trail. In rural areas, the population is more conservative and people are accustomed to modest clothing, especially on women.

Care should be taken to dress modestly when visiting places of worship. If visiting in the winter (May to October), be prepared for cooler temperatures and bring a light jacket or cardigan for the evenings. If you like to dress in an alternative or eccentric way, expect glances and perhaps heckling from across the street.

chapter six

TIME OUT

Thanks to the large number of public holidays, generous arrangements for paid annual leave, and shorter working hours than in many other countries, Mauritians have ample opportunity to enjoy their free time. This is mostly spent with family and close friends, either eating and watching television at home or visiting one of the many attractions across the island. Mauritian men are avid football (soccer) supporters and follow British and European clubs on television.

Although many men drink at local bars, and teenagers and young adults enjoy going to concerts, bars, clubs, and the cinema, Mauritian culture doesn't place great emphasis on "going out." Conservative attitudes mean that coming home late may not be tolerated by one's family, especially in the case of young women.

THE BEACH, BUNGALOW, AND PICNIC

When they have a long weekend, Mauritians take the opportunity to get together and enjoy themselves in the sun. This usually involves trips to the beach or to one of the many small islands just off the coast, like Île aux Cerfs to the east. Extended families often make a big deal of this and arrange a large picnic or barbecue, with soft drinks and activities to occupy the whole family. This serves as a time to share news and to bond in an environment outside the confines of the home. Affluent families will rent a bungalow on the coast and make the most of the location to swim, enjoy water sports, and explore the local area.

When visiting coastal areas yourself, you should be aware that nudity is against the law and that topless sunbathing is not usually tolerated in areas other than beaches owned by hotels.

NATURE AND THE OUTDOORS

Although Mauritians are generally risk averse, many enjoy discovering their natural environment. Trips may be arranged to hike in the Black River Gorges National Park, or to climb one of the many oddly shaped mountains—such as Le Pouce, Corps de Garde, and Lion Mountain—whose summits offer beautiful views across the island. Many visit the botanical gardens in Pamplemousses and Curepipe for the delightful array of tropical flora, or watch wildlife at sanctuaries such as Casela Bird Park. Others simply enjoy going out for a drive to get away from claustrophobic towns.

MAURITIAN CUISINE

Mauritian cuisine has a distinctively mixed and inventive quality. Local dishes—often casseroles or curries—take the traditions of South Asia, Africa, China, and Europe and add a unique Mauritian twist, using delicious local ingredients such as spices, fresh vegetables, exotic fruits, fish, and seafood. Many meals combine the different culinary traditions—Chinese noodle soup, followed by Indian curry with a Creole garnish, and then a French-style tart and *café au lait* would not be uncommon. Mauritians of all backgrounds like to explore different foods and will savor dishes typically associated with other communities, showing how much of a hybrid this society is and how open the population is to its varied traditions.

Staple Foods

The staple food is white rice (boiled, fried, or spiced), imported from Asian countries and served with all types of food. Another starchy staple is Chinese noodles (*minn*). Evening meals in Mauritius tend to be served in copious amounts, so you won't go hungry during your visit.

Meat, fish, seafood, and vegetables are usually served in a curry (*kari*, sometimes on banana leaves), stew, or casserole. Dishes commonly make use of *rougay* (pronounced "roo-guy"), a sauce made from tasty local tomatoes (*pomdamour*), garlic, onion, ginger, and chilies. *Vinnday* (pronounced "vin-die") is a spicy sauce made with vinegar, mustard seeds, and turmeric. *Daube* is a stew using onions, garlic, herbs, and tomatoes.

Fish and seafood feature in many popular dishes, especially *pwason sale* (salted fish), smoked marlin, oysters, shrimps, prawns, and octopus. Monkey curry, bat curry, fried wasp grubs, and marinated *tang* or *tenrec* (a type of hedgehog native to Madagascar, hunted in May) are rarer delicacies that will take Westerners by surprise.

Curry No. 2

Monkey curry—known locally as Curry No. 2—is one of the rarer and more peculiar local dishes. The dish makes use of the local macaque (*zako* in Kreol), introduced to Mauritius by seventeenth-century Dutch sailors and now found in forests across the island. The meat is marinated in garlic, ginger, cinnamon, and white wine before being cooked in masala, tamarind, and coriander.

With two-thirds of the population being of South Asian ancestry, food from this part of the world is a major component of the aromatic Mauritian cuisine. Chilies and spices such as cardamom, turmeric, cloves, and saffron are found in many dishes. *Briani* is a typical Muslim dish, combining rice, onions, spices, potatoes, and meat; it is common for Mauritians of all communities to eat this dish on special occasions such as weddings.

South Asian flat breads such as *naans*, *rotis*, and *faratas* are ubiquitous.

The Chinese influence can be seen in the use of fresh, fried vegetables and oyster and soy sauces. Soups, fried rice, noodles, and *boulet* (dumplings) are served with numerous meat, fish, and vegetable accompaniments. *Bol renversé* ("upside-down bowl") is a dish made with rice and topped with meat or a fried egg. An excellent place to sample Chinese cuisine is Chinatown in Port Louis, and there are many good local Chinese restaurants.

French traditions can be found in classical *haute cuisine* and the use of game such as locally hunted wild boar and venison.

The cuisine of Rodrigues is largely Creole and uses a large amount of local fish, seafood (including octopus), fresh fruit and vegetables, pulses, corn, and beans.

Fresh Fruit and Vegetables

There is an abundance of tropical fruit on the island, and many families have mango, longane

(similar to a lychee), and coconut trees growing in their front or back yards. Lychees, guavas, pineapples, papayas, and bananas are also widely available. Local vegetables include *chou chou* (choyotte), *lalo* (lady's finger), and *brinzel* (a type of eggplant). Sauces and condiments such as *zasar* (or *achards*, pickled vegetables) and *satini* (or *chatini*, chutney) make use of lots of local ingredients and offer a spicy dimension to any dish. Many dishes are also served with *bred* (or *brèdes*, boiled leaves). "Millionaire's Salad," made with heart of palm, fish, and seafood, is a local specialty.

Sweets and Desserts

French-style cakes, pancakes, and pastries are popular. *Napolitaines* are sweet, round cakes with pink icing. Indian sweets (using milk, syrup, and exotic fruits) and Chinese "wax cakes" are eaten by all communities, the latter especially at Chinese New Year. *Poudinn may* (corn pudding) is a popular Creole desert. Delicious local fruits are often served with cream, sorbet, or ice cream, and the more humble yogurt is often referred to using the name of the French brand Yoplait. Flavored manioc cookies are produced by Rault (located near Mahébourg) and are often served with tea.

Street Food

Mauritians also enjoy snacking between meals. Snacks, or *gajak*, can be bought from stalls and street vendors in all the major towns and villages. Street food is eaten as a simple light snack, or sometimes as a worker's lunch. For a small price you can buy delights such as *dal pouri* (spicy lentil and vegetable pancakes), *gato piman* (deep-fried balls of split peas with chili), and *samousa* (pastries stuffed with spicy meat or vegetables). Chinese soup, dumplings, and noodles are also widely available from street vendors, as are sweet snacks such as pineapple spirals and fresh fruit. Although hygiene isn't always a priority for street vendors, these foods can be much more interesting than those found in the Western fast-food chains.

LOCAL DRINKS

Local teas and infusions are well liked and widely available. Vanilla, coconut, and other fruit teas are produced by companies such as Bois Chéri. Coffee is produced locally at Chamarel, and Western-style coffees are popular among the middle classes.

Soft Drinks

Blessed with an ample supply of tropical fruits, Mauritius is home to some refreshing nonalcoholic drinks. Street vendors at beaches and in the towns will cut a coconut open in front of you, so that you can drink the milky juice with a straw. Tropical fruit juices are also widely available. Other, more elaborate concoctions include *alouda*, best sampled at one of the stalls at the Central Market in Port Louis. This is a sweet, refreshing drink combining milk, water, basil seeds, rose syrup, vanilla, and almond essence. The recipe is often adapted to a person's taste, with many adding sauce and ice cream.

Soft drinks such as cola are popular at home and on special occasions. One Mauritian brand, *Eski*, offers interesting, exotic flavors such as almond and vanilla.

Alcoholic Drinks

For lovers of alcohol, Mauritius offers some nice surprises. Foreign drinks can be rather expensive due to the high import levy, but local alcohol is affordable and very good if one chooses wisely.

Local cane rum (such as Green Island) is often mixed with ice and cola, coconut milk, or fruit juices to create wonderful exotic cocktails. *Rhum arrangé* involves placing flavorful fruits and spices in the rum to ferment for weeks or months.

The Phoenix Brewery has been producing good-quality beers since the early 1960s. Phoenix (pronounced "fen-eeks") is a refreshing, award-winning lager (5 percent vol.) that is sold on tap or by the can or bottle. The brand has become something of a national icon, with the advertising line of "*Nou pays, nou labière*" ("Our country, our beer") becoming synonymous with the drink. Blue Marlin is the stronger, heavier sister of Phoenix (6 percent vol.).

For those who can afford it, imported whiskey is very popular, and French and South African wines are fashionable.

Alcohol Abuse
It is not uncommon to see lone, drunk men wandering the streets in Mauritius, whose condition is often the consequence of unemployment and poverty. With a view to combating the high rate of alcohol abuse in Mauritian society and the prevalence of alcohol-related illnesses and social problems, the Public Health Act of March 2009 prohibited the drinking of alcohol in public places and restricted alcohol-related advertising. The minimum age for buying alcohol (and tobacco) is currently eighteen.

RESTAURANTS

The multicultural, creative character of the local cuisine has attracted big international names to open restaurants at hotels and resorts on the island. Mauritians do not eat out very often themselves, however, preferring to save the money and to maintain the importance of family meals at home.

Many non-resort restaurants close by 10:00 or 11:00 p.m., and service can vary widely, ranging from sophisticated French-style waiting (with an attitude) in former colonial estates to a more rustic, down-to-earth experience in local, family-run Creole restaurants. Some restaurants offer a range of dishes from the French, Chinese, Creole, and Indian traditions, whereas others specialize in a particular ethnic cuisine. Grand Baie and Port Louis are the best places to go for a wide choice of different eateries (even Italian and Japanese), whereas other areas are better for particular dishes (the southwest for typical Creole fare, for example). Chinese restaurants in Mauritius often employ staff with no particular Chinese connection.

Vegans and Vegetarians

Only a few Mauritians, but especially Hindus, are vegetarians. Nevertheless, while the country is not particularly geared toward vegans and vegetarians, there are plenty of options for people who do not eat meat or dairy products. For a start, there are plenty of fresh fruits and vegetables, which can easily be combined with rice and other staples; a number of curries, casseroles, bean dishes, and salads are also meat-free.

TIPPING

In restaurants the statutory 15 percent VAT may be added only when you receive your bill. If a service charge has not already been included in the bill, a tip of around 10 percent is expected but is not obligatory. Tipping is less common in cafés and bars and for taxi drivers, but a few coins are fine if you have received exceptional service. It is usual to tip airport porters and hotel room staff around Rs50 or 100. Outside the tourist areas, however, tipping is not common among Mauritians themselves, so hairdressers, laundresses, and tailors won't be angry if you leave without showing your appreciation.

Smoking Ban
In March 2009, the Public Health Act made it illegal to smoke in enclosed public places. As a result you will not be able to smoke in cafés, restaurants, bars, and nightclubs.

THE MUSIC OF MAURITIUS
Music is part of everyday life. Although French, British, and American pop music has been around since the 1960s, the island also has its own

popular folk music, sega, which attracts a great deal of attention and is likely to come up in conversations. Indian and Chinese music can also be heard in daily life and on special occasions.

There are many record shops in Mauritius, such as Harbour Music in Port Louis and Rose Hill, and market stalls across the island. Much recent output is also available online, but fans are encouraged to pay for their music in order to ensure that local artists make a good living.

Sega

Sega, pronounced "say-gah," is the local, rhythmic folk music of Mauritius. It emerged from the songs

and dances performed by African and Malagasy slaves, but also combines elements of European musical traditions such as the polka and quadrille. The name is likely to come from a Bantu verb meaning to play, dance, or enjoy, and similar words are found among the African diaspora in parts of South America and the Caribbean. Traditional sega (*sega tipik*) was performed around a fire, often in the mountains, forests, and beaches in far southwestern Mauritius.

Three percussion instruments are typically used: the *ravann* (a large goatskin drum with cymbals attached to its wooden frame), the *maravann* (a box filled with seeds, which is shaken), and the *triang* or *matriang* (a metal triangle). Other instruments are improvised—pans, cooking utensils, and items found near the beach such as pieces of wood and coconut shells. Instruments were traditionally "tuned" by warming them over a fire. Nowadays, instruments such as drums, horns, synthesizers, and electric guitars are used to great effect.

Many male singers now wear knee-length shorts or pants and brightly colored shirts, and the female dancers wear long, colorful skirts and skimpy tops. Large straw hats are also a common sight. The tempo of a song speeds up while the agile, flirtatious dancing partners—with arms outstretched—move increasingly closer together (without touching), until an ecstatic crescendo is reached in a suggestive pose on the ground. So intoxicating is the sound and the climax, a Mauritian saying states that "Sega is rum that is drunk with the eyes and the ears."

The lyrics, in Kreol, were originally a vehicle to spread news and protest around the island. Today they are often playful and sometimes suggestively sexual. Other common themes include love, courtship, politics, peace, cultural diversity, and *nu zanset* (our ancestors), often a melancholic account of the pain and injustice suffered during slavery and indenture. When a singer chants—almost yodels—the sounds "oh-la-la-eh-la-la-eh!" or any combination of short vowels and consonants, it is an invitation for the musicians to speed up and all those present to join in.

Sega has developed into a form of popular music played by *ségatiers* (sega performers) at hotels and weddings across the island, but also in Rodrigues, Réunion, and the Seychelles. This musical genre can be said to be an authentic, unifying force in the multiethnic societies of the Indian Ocean. It was popularized in Mauritius by artists such as Ti Frère and Serge Lebrasse between the 1950s and 1970s. After this, musicians such as Claudio, Jean-Claude, husband-wife duo Marie-Josée and Roger Clency, and Babalé continued to develop the genre, while others from the poor suburbs of Port Louis developed a more politicized style (*séga engagé*). Artists since the 1990s have experimented with foreign musical influences to create inspirational sounds such as seggae (a marriage of sega and reggae, pioneered by Kaya and his band Racinetatane), sagga (sega and ragga), and seggaemuffin. Popular acts today include Linzy Bacbotte, Ravannes Sans Frontières, Cassiya, and Alain Ramanisum. Repetitive medleys (*popouri*) are played on Mauritian radio and television.

Indian Music
Traditional Indian music using sitars and tablas is popular on the island. Bollywood music is also an inspiration to many Indo-Mauritians, and to others too. In rural areas, and also on radio and television, Mauritian Bhojpuri songs have been the traditional staple and are now acquiring more modern forms. The Bhojpuri Boys combine Bhojpuri traditions and sega to create an innovative musical style.

Opera
A recent arrival on the cultural scene is the Opera Mauritius Festival, which is held each September at venues across the island and uses the talents of a diverse range of local and international singers,

dancers, and musicians. Opera has yet to capture the imagination of the wider Mauritian public.

The presence of opera on the island goes back to the nineteenth century, when European companies would visit Mauritius to perform at the historic Port Louis Theatre. In the twentieth century, the Plaza in Rose Hill was a popular venue for opera and theater, but it is currently under renovation.

ARTS AND CULTURE

The arts are promoted by the Ministry of Arts and Culture. Other nonprofit organizations, like the Fondation Spectacles et Cultures, promote cultural events. As you might expect, cultural life in Mauritius is dominated by multiculturalism. A number of local and national organizations promote French, South Asian, Chinese, and African cultures; these include the Institut Français de Maurice, the Alliance Française, the Indira Gandhi Centre for Indian Culture, the Islamic Cultural Centre, and the Nelson Mandela Centre for African Culture. The British Council in Rose Hill provides cultural events and English-language courses.

An organization called Rezo Otayo-Otébiyé provides listings and sells tickets for a variety of cultural events across the island, and includes a French-language magazine, *Ayo'Culture. Island Info* is a free monthly English-language listings magazine distributed locally and available online.

Theater and Cinema

There are theaters in Vacoas, Mahébourg, and a number of other places. While audiences are mainly the urban middle classes, the productions are not just highbrow imports but include local expressions of the Creole and Indo-Mauritian sensibilities. Playwrights,

such as Dev Virahsawmy, have used the medium to denounce neocolonialism and communalism.

Cinemas tend to screen films from the United States, Europe, China, and the Indian subcontinent. English-language films are generally dubbed in French. Indian films are always popular among Indo-Mauritians, who often watch them without subtitles. A small Mauritian film industry has produced some acclaimed films such as *Bénarès* (2006, adapted from a book of the same name by Barlen Pyamootoo). The Mauritian Île Courts festival and the Festival International du Film d'Afrique et des Îles (in Réunion) promote local films and documentaries.

Mauritian Literature

Despite its small size, Mauritius has been a hub of literary activity in the Indian Ocean since the arrival of the island's first printing press in 1768. Early works, such as Frenchman Bernardin de St. Pierre's well-known classic *Paul et Virginie* (1787), focused on the ideas of love and morality on a tropical island. Robert-Edward Hart (1891–1954) was a Franco-Irish-Mauritian who wrote poetry in French. Malcolm de Chazal (1902–81) was a hugely influential writer, aphorist, poet, and artist who focused on the strange and spiritual essence of the Mauritian natural world.

The Written Word

Referring to the popularity and prestige of the literary professions in his country, Mauritian writer Yvan Lagesse once remarked that "Mauritius has a million inhabitants and just as many writers."

Recent literary works—novels, plays, and poetry, in Hindi, Kreol, and English, but mostly in French—demonstrate the multiplicity of voices and views on the island. A common theme is the history of Mauritius and the quest to understand its cultural identity. While the book market here is small, readers can be found abroad, particularly in Francophone countries. Contemporary Mauritian writers in the Francophone tradition include Ananda Devi, Natacha Appanah-Mouriquand, Carl de Souza, Vinod Rughoonundun, Alain Gordon-Gentil, and Barlen Pyamootoo.

Dev Virahsawmy has been a powerhouse in Kreol literature and has written a huge corpus of poetry, theater, and adaptations of Shakespeare's plays such as *Zeneral Makbef* (*Macbeth*). Many poets writing in Kreol are becoming increasingly popular. Abhimanyu Unnuth is the most widely known Mauritian writing in Hindi, and others such as Lindsey Collen write in English.

The main literary event is the annual Prince Maurice Prize for literary love stories. Prizes are awarded for works written in French and English on alternate years. Other prizes are awarded by international Francophone organizations and literary bodies in the Indian Ocean region.

THE SIRANDANE, OR MAURITIAN RIDDLE

Everyday Mauritian speech is rich in sayings, proverbs, and tales. One genre, the *sirandane*, the Mauritian Kreol riddle, has its roots in the oral culture of former slaves and settlers and can also be found on other islands of the western Indian Ocean. The *sirandane* (sometimes called *zedmo*) contains elements of poetry and wordplay. In a game of question and response participants turn aspects of everyday life into something magical and bizarre. Plants, animals, humans, and nature are the raw materials for this topsy-turvy world of guesswork.

The genre follows a specific structure, with one person opening with the question "*Sirandann?*" and another replying "*Sanpek!*". The riddle—often humorous, sometimes cruel and subversive—then begins.

Tapi mo gran papa plin pinez? Zetwal.
My grandfather's rug is full of drawing pins? The stars.

Piti kuman mo piti, mo fer kone tu mo pwisens? Piman.
Small as I am, I let my strength be known? A chili pepper.

Kan gran maman nwar santé, tu piti blan danse? Duri dan marmit.
When a black grandmother sings, all the little white folk dance? A pot of rice on the cooktop.

[Cited in *Sirandanes*, a collection of these riddles by Nobel Prize-winner Jean-Marie Gustave Le Clézio and his wife, Jémia.]

Visual Arts and Crafts

Painting and other forms of visual art tend to focus on the island's natural history, often presenting its flora and fauna in vibrant, abstract ways. Other subjects include the daily lives of Mauritians. Among the most famous Mauritian artists are Hervé Masson (1919–90), Max Boullé (1899–1965), Malcolm de Chazal (1902–81), and Vaco Baissac (1940–). Although art here has traditionally been European in nature, local modern artists have been forging a new and challenging body of work.

Sculpture has been used to great effect to commemorate public and religious figures. Prosper d'Épinay (1836–1914) was the first leading exponent of Mauritian sculpture.

Popular art forms include woodwork and handicrafts, such as jewelry, ornaments, model ships, and the ubiquitous carvings of the dodo.

SHOPPING FOR PLEASURE

Mauritian markets can be exciting places, where the hustle and bustle combines with exotic aromas to create a heady atmosphere. Haggling is expected and the islanders are renowned for their love of a bargain (you will hear the words *bon marsé* a great deal, meaning that a product is cheap). If a price is not displayed and you decide to haggle, be aware that Mauritians will rise to the challenge. It's worth suggesting a significantly lower price than what you expect to pay, if only to ensure that you leave with some spare change. Useful phrases include "*Comié sa?*" ("How much is it?") and "*Sa pa bon marsé!*" ("It's not cheap!").

Popular markets (*bazars* or *foires*) can be found in the main towns. There is a daily market in Port Louis (open 6:00 a.m. to 6:00 p.m.), but other markets only open on certain days.

You are more than likely to encounter hawkers (*marsan ambulan*) selling goods as varied as snacks, refreshing drinks, trinkets, jewelry, maps, clothing, and sunglasses. Handicrafts are found in specialty shops, such as those at the Craft Market at the

Caudan Waterfront complex in Port Louis. Shops in Port Louis are normally open from 9:00 a.m. to 5:00 p.m. during the week and until noon on Saturdays. In central plateau towns such as Curepipe and Quatre Bornes, shops might open at the slightly later time of 10:00 a.m. and close at 5:30 p.m. Many shops close early at lunchtime on Thursdays and Sundays. VAT of 15 percent applies to most goods and services.

Currency

The Mauritian rupee (Rs or MUR) is divided into 100 cents, or *sous*). Coins appear in denominations of 1, 5, 10, and 20 rupees, and there are also notes to the value of 25, 50, 100, 200, 500, 1,000, and 2,000 rupees. The banknotes carry the image of an historical figure or a Mauritian landmark, with values in English, Tamil, and Hindi, and a watermark in the shape of a dodo.

SPORTS

Mauritians are passionate about sports, but despite ample opportunity to participate in them, either at sports centers or on the beach, the islanders tend not to be very active themselves. For many, sports are for watching, not playing, evident in the low ranking of the national teams and the disproportionate popularity of successful Western sportspeople. Due to the prohibitive cost, some games, such as golf, tend to be played solely by tourists and the wealthy elite. Boxer Bruno Julie became the first ever Mauritian Olympic medalist, winning a bronze medal in Beijing in 2008.

Football

Soccer is a national obsession. Club shirts are worn on streets across the island, posters and memorabilia are found inside cars and homes, and flags are tied to trees in people's yards. It is, however, European football that really gets the adrenalin pumping. English Premier League teams are followed closely on national television and in local newspapers. The celebrity of European football contrasts sharply with the Mauritian game, where national players are semiprofessional and local teams struggle to attract supporters into their stadiums.

Interethnic violence associated with football cast a dark shadow over the game in the late 1960s and again in the late 1990s, prompting the authorities to ban many matches and prevent clubs from being formed on an ethnic basis. Although supposedly fairer now, the new rules have resulted in a lack of rivalry between teams and a severe loss of interest in local football. Club M—or Les Dodos, as the national team is known unofficially—has never qualified for the World Cup finals.

Horse Racing

Another very popular sport is horse racing, which allows Mauritians to indulge their love of gambling. The prestigious Champ de Mars racecourse in Port Louis is set in a natural amphitheater of green hills and mountains, and is the oldest racecourse in the Southern Hemisphere, having been founded by the Mauritius Turf Club in 1812. Jockeys and horses are drawn to the venue from around the world. Races are held on weekends from May to December, sometimes attracting as many as 50,000 spectators.

Water Sports

There are ample facilities for waterskiing, windsurfing, kitesurfing, sailing, and sea kayaking, which can often be organized by hotels or specialty companies (check that they hold permits issued by the Ministry of Tourism). Diving and snorkeling offer a fascinating glimpse of the island's coral reef, tropical fish, and marine life, and a boat trip to the many smaller islands makes an exciting excursion. Certain coastal areas are protected marine parks where nature should not be disturbed. Also, when participating in water sports, you should protect your feet against coral and venomous stonefish.

La Regatta

The Regatta is an annual sailing competition showcasing the traditional, flat-bottomed wooden pirogue in the historic bay at Mahébourg. This boat is also used by local Creole fishermen.

Other Sports

For serious runners there is the Royal Raid, a grueling cross-country race held every May, and the Marathon de l'Île Maurice, which follows the picturesque coastline of southwest Mauritius. If you prefer jogging, there is plenty of opportunity to exercise in areas of outstanding natural beauty.

Mauritius offers perfect terrain for cycling and mountain biking, from the flat land of the north, where roads are lined with fields of sugarcane, to coastal roads and the rugged interior of the central plateau and the Black River Gorges.

Rugby Union is popular mainly among Franco-Mauritians. Deer hunting is almost exclusively a Franco-Mauritian pastime.

Gambling

Gambling is extremely popular, especially among men. There are several casinos on the island, mainly in Port Louis, Curepipe, and the tourist areas, where there are slot machines and gamblers can play roulette, blackjack, and poker into the early hours of the morning, taking in a few drinks at the casino bar. Mauritians place bets on horses running at the Champ de Mars and buy tickets for the Mauritius Lottery, and informal gambling also takes place among friends and colleagues.

chapter seven

TRAVEL, HEALTH, & SAFETY

Mauritius is geared toward high-end tourism, which is carefully developed and managed by the government. The five-star hotels and tourist infrastructure make it a destination of choice for cash-rich Westerners and couples looking for a romantic honeymoon idyll. Despite it being an expensive destination to reach, foreign currency makes Mauritius a cheap place to be once you have arrived, and there is plenty here to keep you relaxed and occupied.

The real Mauritius, however, away from the tourist areas, is much more challenging than you might expect. The roads are chaotic, and in the towns the combination of congestion, heat, and social tension can cause aggression. A minority of Mauritians do not really live up to the country's reputation for warmth and hospitality.

RED TAPE

Visas are not required to enter Mauritius if you have a valid US, EU, Canadian, Australian, New Zealand, or South African passport. For requirements for other nationalities, visit the Mauritius Passport and Immigration Office on the government Web site at www.gov.mu. Visitors are usually permitted to stay up to a month, providing they have arranged accommodation, sufficient funds, and a return ticket or evidence of onward travel. If you want to stay any longer, you have to obtain an extended visa and a residence permit from the Passport and Immigration Office.

There are restrictions on importing plants, animals, and medicines, and limits on tobacco, alcohol, and perfume. It is illegal to import cigarette papers. Customs officers are respectful, but can turn tough if you don't abide by the rules.

FLIGHTS

Flights from many major international airports arrive at Sir Seewoosagur Ramgoolam International Airport, near Mahébourg. The country's own airline, Air Mauritius, offers a number of internal and external services. Arriving by plane is a breathtaking experience, with spectacular views of the beautiful blue lagoons, the lush, green interior of the island, and its oddly shaped volcanic peaks. There are no direct flights from North America, so visitors usually fly via London or Paris. Flights from the UK take around twelve hours and range from £600 to £1,000 (US$950–$1,500) for a round-trip ticket, depending on the season. The most economical way of traveling to Mauritius is to buy a package deal from a tour operator, including flights and accommodation.

TRAVEL TO RÉUNION, RODRIGUES, AND THE OUTER ISLANDS

Air Mauritius offers fast services to Réunion and Rodrigues (to Sir Gaëtan Duval Airport at Plaine

Corail, one and a half hours), and Air Austral also flies to Réunion. Ferry services between Mauritius and Réunion are operated by the Mauritius

Shipping Corporation a couple of times a week, with journey times taking about eleven hours. Rodrigues can be reached by ferry on a thirty-six-hour journey (two or three times a month).

Rodrigues

Unlike Mauritius itself, Rodrigues is still relatively undisturbed by tourism. There is, however, a growing interest in ecotourism on the island. There are some decent hotels, and guest houses are available. Shops and services are also said to close by 4:00 p.m., and the island has only one gas station.

Cargados Carajos Shoals (Saint Brandon)

It is very rare for anyone other than fishermen and state employees to visit these islands. Anyone who does so must stomach an eighteen-hour journey by boat and potentially wet and windy weather conditions when they arrive. There is very little in the way of local amenities, save for lodging barracks and a community hall.

Agalega

Travel to Agalega can be organized only by the Mauritian Outer Islands Development Corporation, and is mostly restricted to people working on the islands. There is a twice-yearly ferry trip on the *Mauritius Pride*, and irregular, three-hour flights of dubious comfort and safety can be arranged with the Mauritian Coast Guard. Some basic amenities exist on the islands, including a shop, a post office, and a bank.

PUBLIC TRANSPORTATION

There has been no rail network in Mauritius since the 1950s. As a result, public transportation is largely restricted to buses and coaches—a combination of sleek, professional, air-conditioned commuter services and ramshackle, crowded buses operated by local family businesses. Many people rely on these services for school, work, and shopping. By using buses in Mauritius, you will have the opportunity to meet many warm, colorful characters whom you wouldn't come across if you stuck to using taxis. You'll hear the magical Kreol language in full use and you'll catch a glimpse of the daily lives of ordinary people.

There is good coverage of towns and villages across the island provided by a network of public and private bus companies, including the National Transport Corporation (NTC), United Bus Service (UBS), Rose Hill Transport (RHT), Mauritius Bus Transport (MTB), and Triolet Bus Service (TBS). Though many routes wind through residential and commercial areas, there are also express services between the main bus depots of local towns and the capital. Most destinations on the island can be reached in an hour or two, often involving transfers. If you want to stop in a rural area, this is usually by request only.

Many services start early, at 5:30 a.m., but they finish early too, at least by European standards. If you don't intend to take a taxi, you'll need to ensure that you catch the last bus home before around 6:30 p.m. in rural areas and 8:00 p.m. in town. There is one late-night service (until 11:00 p.m.!) between the capital and the central plateau towns. It is better to avoid traveling during peak times (between 8:00 and 9:00 a.m., and also in the late afternoon) on commuter journeys to and from Port Louis. Tickets are bought from the conductor (*kontroler*) after you have boarded the bus and are usually very cheap—from Rs5 for local trips to anywhere up to Rs120 for longer journeys. Try to pay in small change rather than with notes.

TAXIS

A more comfortable way of getting around is by taxi, although this isn't always affordable for many islanders. Using taxis gives you the flexibility to visit places off the beaten path and to stop off at places en route. Cabs are sometimes unmetered, but can be relatively cheap if you negotiate a good deal beforehand. A short journey from one town to another might cost in the region of Rs200 to 400. If you feel like having your own personal guide, a taxi driver might be happy to offer you a day's tour of the island for around Rs2,000 to 2,500. Beware of unlicensed taxis (*taxi maron*) and others "taking you for a ride" by soliciting your patronage in various shops owned by friends and relatives.

Way Out in the Center

A common joke told by taxi drivers is that in Mauritius they do not drive on the left or the right, but in the middle.

DRIVING

Mauritians, like the British, drive on the left. The regulations and road signs could lead you to believe that you are driving in a strange, tropical version of the United Kingdom, but the

comparisons stop there. Driving in Mauritius can be a dangerous activity, especially considering the poor upkeep of the roads in towns and the tendency of pedestrians to stray into the traffic. Nevertheless, driving can be extremely enjoyable if you are alert to the many hazards. There is some beautiful scenery along the coastal roads and in rural areas.

Mauritius has around 1,250 miles (2,000 km) of surfaced road, forming a continuous highway between the southeast and the resorts in the far north of the island. This "highway," perhaps a misnomer, varies widely in character from two or three lanes separated by a grass shoulder to a single lane more akin to a local road. The remaining road network is comprised of primary and secondary highways and many smaller rural roads, many of which are off-limits because they are reserved for the use of sugar plantations.

The minimum age for driving is eighteen for cars, seventeen for motorcycles, and fifteen for mopeds. Foreigners are allowed to drive in Mauritius providing they hold a valid driver's license in their country of residence.

You might want to borrow a car from a Mauritian friend or rent one from one of the many rental firms at the airport, Port Louis, and the central plateau towns (at least Rs1,000 per day is normal, and you usually have to be at least twenty-three years old).

ADVICE FOR DRIVERS

- Speed limits are given in kilometers. They are 25 to 37 mph (40 to 60 kmph) in built-up areas, 50 mph (80 kmph) out of town, and 56 mph (90 kmph) on freeways. Mobile speed traps are used on main roads and freeways.
- Passing is on the right.
- Keep a full tank when driving into rural areas: there might not be a gas station for miles around. Gas stations are manned by attendants who will fill up your tank for you. It is not customary to tip attendants.
- Due to narrow streets and congestion, it is advisable to use off-street parking garages where possible.
- Seat belts are compulsory, and drunk driving is forbidden. Alcohol limits are 23 micrograms in 100 ml of breath, 50 milligrams in 100 ml of blood, or 67 milligrams in 100 ml of urine. This is roughly the equivalent of one shot of whiskey or rum, one pint of lager, or one glass of wine.
- Beware of a lack of street lighting at night, passing taxis and buses, heavily laden trucks, blind corners, potholes, and storm drains close to the curb.
- Look out for wandering pedestrians, cyclists, and stray dogs, both on narrow local streets and on the main roads and freeways.
- If you are involved in a serious road accident, it would be wise to call the police as soon as possible as there have been incidents of ugly scenes developing.

SOLO
Hitchhiking
Hitchhiking is uncommon among Mauritians (they are more likely to share a ride with a neighbor or a colleague), but some tourists enjoy getting around this way. It can be a pleasant way to meet local people and experience life as they see it. However, due care should be taken not to put yourself in danger by traveling alone (especially if you are a woman), and you have been warned about the nature of driving in Mauritius.

Cycling
Cycling is a cheap and enjoyable way of exploring the island's beautiful landscapes, but can be extremely dangerous. A large proportion of the accidents on Mauritian roads involve cars colliding with cyclists and pedestrians. Bikes can be rented from large hotels and local tour operators.

WHERE TO STAY
Accommodation in Mauritius is skewed toward luxury options in the coastal areas. Modest alternatives include cheaper hotels, guest houses (*chambres d'hôte*) where you can get closer to locals and experience daily life, or self-catering bungalows and other properties. When choosing where to stay, ensure that your hotel or rented accommodation is registered with the Ministry of Tourism. Three main areas cater to tourists: the north around Grand Baie and Pereybère, the west coast from Flic en Flac down to Le Morne, and the east and southeast from Belle Mare to Blue Bay.

Accommodation on Rodrigues is usually low-key and modest in comparison with Mauritius, since expensive hotels have yet to arrive. Here, you are much more likely to stay with a local family and eat at the table with them.

If you are looking for long-term rentals, it is a good idea to consult local real estate agents or look at advertisements in newspapers such as *Le Mauricien* and *L'Express*. You will be expected to pay a deposit along with your rent, which tends to be cheaper in the central plateau area. Many properties are furnished.

PLACES TO VISIT

Mauritius can be explored fully in around two to three weeks. There is a wide range of activities on offer for tourists. Here are some of the highlights.

- Trips to beaches around Grand Baie, Flic en Flac, Le Morne, Blue Bay, and Belle Mare, and boat trips to islands such as Île aux Cerfs (east coast) and Îlot Gabriel (north coast).
- Diving, snorkeling, and water sports at many locations around the island.
- Hiking in the Black River Gorges National Park and the Domaine du Chasseur, and climbing one of the island's many mountains.

- Walking in gardens and wildlife sanctuaries such as the SSR Botanical Gardens in Pamplemousses, Casela Nature Park, and La Vanille Crocodile Park.

- Trips to spacious colonial residences such as Eureka (near Moka).
- Trips to historic sites and monuments at Le Morne, Vieux Grand Port, and Cap Malheureux.
- Visiting Port Louis, the central plateau towns, and Mahébourg for shops, markets, architecture, and museums.
- A short trip to Rodrigues for a more relaxed pace of life.

The Mauritius Tourism Promotion Authority (MPTA, www.tourism-mauritius.mu) has offices around the island and in several countries around the world. While in Mauritius, you can also receive general tourist information from Mauritius Telecom by dialing 152.

HEALTH

Medicine in Mauritius ranges from Western, European-style hospitals and doctors' offices to Chinese herbalism and Indian Ayurvedic medicine. The national health-care system is free of charge to citizens, and facilities exist in all the main urban areas. Private health care is also available, such as at the modern, high-tech Clinique Darné in Floréal. Such facilities have even given rise to medical tourism. Before traveling, you should arrange travel insurance and research local doctors and hospitals in case of emergencies. Your embassy may have a list of recommended local practitioners.

A common cause of death among Mauritians is heart disease. Around 2 percent of the Mauritian population is thought to be living with HIV, and the number of cases has risen sharply since 2000.

Cases of dengue fever have been reported in the Mascarenes, and in 2005 and 2006 there was a serious outbreak of chikungunya, a mosquito-borne virus causing fever, joint pain, nausea, and rashes. Make sure you use antimosquito products to protect yourself against such viruses. Other than these risks, the only annoyance will be the cockroach, found in homes and hotels throughout Mauritius, upon whose appearance locals will often scream the pest's local name, "kankrela!"

The authorities recommend that you are vaccinated against hepatitis A and B. Water is generally safe to drink but can lead to stomachaches, so bottled water is advisable.

SAFETY
Women
Women travelers should avoid walking alone at night in quiet areas as there have been some reports of assault and rape against tourists. Some travelers, especially women, are the focus of a large amount of staring in the street. This is often harmless, but you may be annoyed at the frequently heard "*Mo mama, o!*" (literally, "Oh, my mother!"), the equivalent of a wolf whistle on the streets of New York or Los Angeles.

LGBT Travelers
Mauritians generally disapprove of same-sex relationships and open displays of homosexuality. This is due in part to the conservative religious background of the large majority of the population, and also to the fact that gossip spreads fast on such a small island where traditional family values rule. "Sodomy" is technically punishable by a five-year prison sentence. As a result, homosexuality has in the past been largely hidden from public view, although LGBT organizations like Collectif Arc-en-Ciel (Rainbow Coalition) and recent antidiscrimination laws are beginning to change this. Some hotels advertise Mauritius as "gay-friendly," but local attitudes suggest the opposite.

Crime
Violent crime is rare in Mauritius, but petty crime is widespread and normally involves theft of bags and valuables in popular tourist areas. Any

valuables should be stored in a safe place before you head out. Many hotels offer the use of a safe, and you should make photocopies of your passport and travel documents. When hiking, use a guide or travel with a group; some unfortunate tourists have been mugged by locals who have taken advantage of their naive view of Mauritians as a peaceful, unaggressive group of people.

Thanks to the action taken by the Mauritian police and many honest locals to eradicate such nuisances, crime is a still only a marginal issue. The Tourist Police (*Police du Tourisme*) has a hotline for anyone who wants to report a crime: 213 2818.

Drugs

A number of illicit recreational drugs are used in Mauritius. Cannabis—known locally as *gandia* or *masse*—is used widely and has been grown illegally in the mountains and sugarcane fields. Heroin is in demand in urban areas. Illicit drugs are not tolerated in Mauritius—there are fines of up to Rs 100,000 and jail sentences of up to five years for possession—so you would be wise to steer clear of traffickers and dealers. An Anti-Drug and Smuggling Unit operates nationwide.

Prostitution

Prostitution is illegal, but exists in areas of Port Louis and other towns. Women, men, and children often fall into prostitution due to poverty. The Ministry of Women's Rights, Family Welfare and Child Development and local NGOs are taking steps to protect victims and reduce prostitution.

NATURAL DISASTERS

Although natural disasters rarely hit the island, a number of tropical cyclones have caused widespread havoc and suffering in Mauritius. Cyclones Carol in 1960, Gervaise in 1975, and Hollanda in 1994 have gone down in history as the most destructive, leaving thousands of residents homeless. These disasters have led to major efforts being made in the building of solid, secure housing. You can receive cyclone reports by dialing 96, and general weather information on 171.

Although northern Mauritius and Rodrigues reported minor flooding and larger-than-average waves, the islands were largely unaffected by the Indian Ocean tsunami in 2004. There is still a risk that Mauritius might be affected by such natural phenomena in the future, however, particularly in vulnerable coastal areas. It is reassuring that much of the population lives at higher altitude on the central plateau and is therefore relatively safe.

EMERGENCY SERVICES
Police
The Mauritius Police Force headquarters can be found at Line Barracks in Port Louis, with a number of branches dealing with drugs and smuggling, investigations, the coast guard, traffic, and passports and immigration. Rodrigues has a separate police force. Police officers generally wear light blue shirts and black flat caps. The police here have often been accused of racism and brutality toward fellow Mauritians, but are generally helpful and respectful to foreigners.

The Special Mobile Force (SMF) is a thousand-strong paramilitary unit employed to ensure internal and external security, and provide help in search and rescue operations, cyclone recovery, and ceremonial guard duties. SMF officers wear camouflage or khaki military-style uniforms, and have a bizarre motto: "We'll do it, what is it?"

The Special Supporting Unit (SSU) is another branch of the police force whose duty it is to control civil unrest and assist in other tasks such as crowd control and escorting dangerous criminals.

Ambulance
The SAMU (Service Aide Médicale Urgence) is the Mauritian ambulance service.

Fire Services
Several of the large towns have a twenty-four-hour fire response unit. Firemen wear brown uniforms with a red belt.

EMERGENCY TELEPHONE NUMBERS	
Emergency services operator	999 or 112
SAMU (ambulance)	114
Fire Services	995 or 115
Cyclone reports	96
Tourist Police	213 1740
	210 3894
Traffic Police	211 8434
	211 8478

chapter eight

BUSINESS BRIEFING

Mauritius has emerged as one of the strongest economies in the Africa–Indian Ocean region and is now attracting investment from around the world. The recent economic downturn took its time to reach the island. As a result, the growth of tourism and the textiles export industry has been checked, and companies on the island have been turning to foreign countries for cheap labor, especially India, Bangladesh, and China.

A young, educated, cosmopolitan, and multilingual workforce means that Mauritians can work quite easily with businesses from Europe, Africa, Asia, and other areas of the world. Gone are the old days of a sugarcane mono-crop

economy. The country now offers a diversified business environment based on sugar, manufacturing, textiles, tourism, and offshore banking. Its stable democracy and free market economy have encouraged many foreign companies to set up shop on the island, and the authorities generally welcome foreign businesses working with Mauritians. This is a safe and stable environment for expats and their families.

The Bank of Mauritius is the country's central bank and regulates the banking sector. The Financial Services Commission regulates the nonbanking financial services sector.

THE BUSINESS CLASSES

Hindus as a group dominate the public sector. Franco-Mauritians and some Indo- and Sino-Mauritians are the undisputed managerial classes in the private sector, especially the sugar, export, and high-end tourism industries.

Middle-class Creoles often fill roles in the media industries, lower managerial positions, and teaching. Creoles (often of discernible African ancestry) and poorer members of other communities are the island's working class, in construction, the docks, workshops, fishing, agriculture, and retail. Manufacturing and textiles are dominated by women from all communities.

Bear in mind that state employees, doctors, lawyers, and university professors command a great deal of respect in Mauritius.

Any foreigner who is equipped with an understanding of Mauritian customs and culture will be warmly welcomed by local businesspeople. To earn their trust it is important to spend some time getting to know them, but you should not get too close or familiar. In some organizations managers will frequently be overworked and unable to respond quickly to your requests.

WORK CULTURE

Most of the population is literate, many are highly skilled, and job satisfaction is important. Management generally provides comfortable and attractive working environments, and some larger companies look after their employees by organizing annual events and providing free transportation to and from work. Employees are usually entitled to fourteen days' paid leave and numerous days of paid "sick leave" per year. This generous approach often results in employee absences typically on either side of a weekend or public holiday.

Despite their communalism outside the workplace, employees from different backgrounds like working together and worker solidarity is strong. Strikes are legal but uncommon. Dozens of powerful trade unions exist in sectors as varied as agriculture, teaching, industry, tourism, and transport, and these are all united under the Mauritius Trade Union Congress. Fierce activism was the norm among the working classes in the 1970s and 1980s, but has declined considerably since Mauritius became more economically stable. Opposing parties today are more likely to engage in mediation to resolve disputes about wages and working conditions.

SETTING UP A MEETING

When submitting bids for business, it is essential to find a useful local contact to help you negotiate your way through the political and social minefields. Such a person could act as your intermediary and even help you deal with legal and administrative matters. Knowing someone from the particular ethno-religious group you are dealing with could provide you with a degree of leverage in establishing business contacts. With the increasingly  global nature of business in Mauritius, however, Mauritian businesspeople are likely to be quite receptive to foreigners investing in and setting up business on the island, and you might be able to avoid the effects of local ethnic rivalries.

When seeking a meeting, it is customary to write a letter or send an e-mail. A degree of formality is required; impeccable Standard English will command respect in dealings with the state sector, while good French will be of benefit when dealing with private companies.

Due to the many public holidays and shorter working hours, it is a good idea to arrange meetings well in advance. Once you have set up a meeting, you will encounter an impressive degree of professionalism from the Mauritians. They are likely to treat you with a good deal of respect and attend to e-mails, correspondence, and telephone calls in an efficient and courteous manner.

Although Mauritians are not generally punctual, punctuality is important in the world of work. Delays are possible, however, if individuals are traveling from another part of the island and using public transportation. You should avoid being late yourself in order to ensure that your professional reputation remains intact.

Businesspeople are rarely on first-name terms, since this is usually considered disrespectful. Instead, Mr., Mrs. or Miss X will generally suffice. Shaking hands is normal practice among the business class, although some Indo-Mauritians are reluctant to shake hands with members of the opposite sex. Male and female colleagues working for informal companies sometimes greet each other with a kiss on each cheek, but this can cause embarrassment in more conservative circles. It is normal practice to exchange business cards and company brochures at meetings.

BUSINESS DRESS
Dressing respectfully means you mean business, so a dark suit and tie would be appropriate for men, and a below-the-knee length skirt and generally modest clothing for women. Don't go over the top, though; individual organizations differ in their approach to dress. Ask about this in advance if you are going to be working with a

company for a substantial period of time. A safe bet for working in an office job would be to wear a shirt, trousers, and tie if you are a man, or a blouse and trousers or formal skirt if you are a woman. Some organizations are much less formal, but this is still not the norm.

PRESENTATIONS

Do not underestimate the experience local businesspeople have of Western business practices. Despite their seeming isolation, Mauritians are cosmopolitan and astute when it comes to dealing with foreigners. Nevertheless, remember to respect the Mauritian brand of multiculturalism in your presentations. Cultural taboos such as ethnicity and sex are best avoided.

French is the language of the business classes, and the ability to present your case in French will take you far. When it comes to the state sector, the ability to present documentation in formal, written English will be a major benefit.

NEGOTIATIONS

A warm, polite, and friendly style in negotiations is appropriate, since this is how Mauritians behave themselves. This warmth should not extend to physical contact, though, and a degree of dignity and reserve is in order. Facial expression and eye contact are important, but not too much, since staring is considered rude and intrusive. You will usually be dealing directly with the decision-maker, but attentive subordinates will also be present, so try to include them in the conversation.

Your attitude should always be respectful, never patronizing, and bear in mind that your counterpart may command a large amount of respect in his or her community. Expect Mauritians to try to bargain for a better deal; this should not be dismissed, but treated as an opportunity to bargain for something else in return.

Once the meeting has ended—and it may take longer than you expect, since Mauritians tend to proceed with caution—it is customary for the host to accompany the guest out of the office and to shake hands. Your host may insist on accompanying you off the premises; you should initially decline the offer before finally accepting.

CONTRACTS AND FULFILLMENT

Broadly speaking, contracts are adhered to in Mauritius, although bureaucracy has been the cause of many a delayed project. Furthermore, although they will try their hardest to complete a project on time, Mauritian employees are unlikely to give up their valued leisure time to work outside office hours. Monitor the progress of any project, otherwise leisurely workers won't take it seriously. Polite, nonconfrontational follow-up e-mails and telephone calls will ensure the work is completed.

When working with Mauritians, remember that discontent can lurk beneath the veneer of politeness and saving face. Try to draw out any issues or misunderstandings at an early stage lest they develop into something more serious later on.

In the event of serious disagreements, the Supreme Court has a specialized commercial division to resolve disputes related to contracts.

BUSINESS ENTERTAINMENT

Many topflight business meetings take place in elegant restaurants and hotels, where comfort and hospitality are the order of the day. Indeed, hospitality and personal relationships are regarded as a means of solidifying and developing a business relationship. Many successful businesses will also offer visitors outings to discover the island's superb natural environment, and bonding exercises might include a round of golf on a luxury golf course.

If you happen to be invited out for a business dinner, it would be unwise to give your host a gift. This is because of the risk of it being interpreted as a bribe, especially if the host has an important position in a state institution. It is normal practice for the host to pay for the meal. If you are invited to the home of a client, however, it is perfectly appropriate to bring something unlikely to be construed as corrupt, such as flowers or, if it is not against their principles, a bottle of wine. In these social situations, care should be taken not to ask questions of a personal nature, especially as regards money, background, or political allegiances.

WOMEN IN BUSINESS

Despite the greater opportunities now available to Mauritian women, Mauritius is still very much a patriarchal society and most businesses are likely to be run by men. Conservative Mauritians feel uneasy about the mixing of the sexes in public life and, consequently, in the world of work. Follow the culture of the people you are dealing with and avoid shaking hands with members of the opposite sex until you are prompted to do so.

If you are a female manager, or at least in a position of responsibility, you are likely to encounter a degree of reticence on the part of male colleagues who are unaccustomed to working under a woman. You should make your role clear from the outset and assert this in order to avoid future misunderstandings.

BUREAUCRACY

The experience of French and British colonial rule has had an impact on the style of administration found in Mauritius. Although this has led to a well organized and mostly efficient system in which you can get things done if you follow the right course, there are a number of impediments to any successful business project. First, you often have only a small window of opportunity to deal with permits and administrative matters in a country where some offices are open for only a few hours each day. Second, the generous number of public holidays often means that meetings and hard work have to be put on hold until a long weekend and a leisurely return to work are out of the way.

The government has recently made huge efforts to ensure that foreign businesses can operate efficiently in the country. The Business Facilitation Act of 2006 is one of several such measures. The government has also created a Work & Live in Mauritius department within the Mauritius Board of Investment in order to speed up the process of settling on the island and setting up a business, which can now take as little as three days and can be as cheap as Rs5,000.

CORRUPTION AND NEPOTISM

All things considered, Mauritians are charming people to do business with and Mauritius offers a very pleasant working environment. However, shady deals do take place on this paradise island. You should be aware of the possibility of corruption and nepotism in the world of work, although this is not as widespread as it once was. Ethnic franchises are common, and some state institutions have a reputation for accepting bribes; nonetheless, the government has taken a stand on these problems by setting up the Independent Commission Against Corruption in 2002.

chapter nine

COMMUNICATING

THE LANGUAGES OF MAURITIUS

Mauritius is a delight to the ears. During
your stay you will hear many languages
spoken around you, testimony to the
country's mixed population and to the
fact that many Mauritians are
multilingual. The prevalence and general
acceptance of multilingualism means that
Mauritians are not offended by hearing a language
they do not understand spoken in the street. The
main languages used in daily life are Kreol, French,
Bhojpuri, and a smattering of English.

The Constitution, written in English, mentions
no official language, although English often fills
this role. French tends to play the prestigious role of
the language of business and culture. It is a bizarre
situation in which English is effectively the official
language but is no one's mother tongue.

Debates about language in Mauritius have
become increasingly controversial in the past few
decades, particularly because language is a status
symbol and an essential part of group identity on
the island. First, French and English continue to
compete with each other, generally with French
coming out on top. Second, Mauritians of Hindu,
Muslim, and Chinese backgrounds have

campaigned successfully for the inclusion of their "ancestral languages" in the education system. These are Hindi, Urdu, Mandarin, and other South Asian and Chinese languages, which may not actually be spoken as first languages by their champions. Kreol-language nationalists, many of whom are actually Indo-Mauritians (see page 151), are becoming increasingly vociferous in their campaign to have Kreol accepted as the national language of the country, while Bhojpuri, the other language traditionally used in rural areas, is losing huge numbers of speakers every year.

It would be useful to arrive on the island with a grounding in French, since this is regarded as the language of commerce, culture, and a sign of education. Apart from government administration and in the main tourist centers, French and Kreol dominate in daily life. Ads and notices often combine French, English, and Kreol. Although Mauritians are used to switching pragmatically between the island's languages, they are not known to be proficient in other foreign languages unless they have spent some time abroad.

English
Although very few people use it in everyday life, the language of officialdom is English. This perhaps serves as a compromise: since English is no one's mother tongue, no one group can feel aggrieved that it has been chosen above any other language.

English is used in most government documents and official communications, and is normally the language spoken in the National Assembly (although French and Kreol are also used to varying degrees). It is also the main language of instruction in state schools. The national anthem is sung in English, and you might even hear people singing "Happy Birthday" or see birthday cards written in English. Some books and newspapers are also published in English, as are many Web sites. The English you read may sometimes appear old-fashioned and stilted.

Nevertheless, English remains marginal in daily life, and many islanders would struggle to hold a decent conversation in it, although the younger, more educated generation are keen to learn it and use it with foreigners.

French

Despite the official nature of English, French is the dominant international language of Mauritius. You are likely to hear it spoken in business and the media, and as a polite language used by strangers trying to show each other respect. Many Mauritians can understand and speak French fluently. In fact, fluency in French has social cachet, due in part to its historical association with the urban middle class. Many Kreol speakers prefer to use French at home with their young children as a way of giving them a head start at school.

The press is dominated by French, as is serious culture and literature. Personal correspondence is often in French, although Kreol is often used in e-mails and text messages. Many cultural organizations (such as the Alliance Française) promote French in Mauritius, and the Francophone nature of the island has allowed Mauritians to bond easily with nationals from countries in the Francophone world.

Kreol (Mauritian Creole)

Kreol is the de facto national language, used in everyday communication between Mauritians of all ethnic, cultural, and religious backgrounds. It is also the mother tongue of more than 75 percent of the population, and not exclusively the Creole ethnic group. To a large extent this flexible and adaptable lingua franca unites the nation. Nevertheless, Kreol is not officially acknowledged.

Kreol developed during French colonial rule as a means of communication between slaves, slave owners, and free islanders, all of whom came from different parts of the world and spoke different languages. Later, under British rule, Indian and Chinese immigrants and indentured laborers found that they, too, were better off using Kreol as a way of communicating with others. Although largely based on French vocabulary, Kreol is now an independent entity and has drawn influences from languages from around the Indian Ocean and the rest of the world. Its grammar does not adhere to French notions of *clarté* and *précision*, but follows its own logic. As a predominantly spoken language devoid of rules dictated from above, Kreol has a raw, earthy feel and is wonderful to hear.

Mauritian Kreol is mutually intelligible with its counterpart spoken in the Seychelles and also with Chagossian Kreol (although with slight differences of accent and vocabulary), but it is quite different and unintelligible to speakers of the creole language spoken in Réunion. Nowadays, many middle-class speakers often use a variety of Kreol that is heavily influenced by French (*kreol fransisé*), a result of the ever-present French influence in Mauritian life.

When choosing whether to use French or Kreol, many Mauritians (especially working-class men) see Kreol as a masculine status symbol as opposed to the supposedly effeminate French language.

Although there has been, and continues to be, a powerful movement promoting Kreol as a fully fledged national language, many Mauritians sadly consider it to be a nonlanguage: a *patois*, a debased, bastardized dialect, or "broken French." Look beyond this Eurocentric embarrassment, however, and you will discover in Kreol a rich, expressive language used by most of the population in everyday life. It is adaptable, flexible, and open to new influences. You can find advertisements, political tracts, poetry, novels, even Shakespeare's *Hamlet*, all written in Kreol, and an oral culture in the form of riddles, songs, and slang show it to be a living, breathing language.

Bhojpuri

Bhojpuri is an Indo-European language spoken by about 37 million people in areas of north and northeast India, predominantly in the states of Bihar, Jharkhand, and Uttar Pradesh. Closely related to Hindi, it was the language spoken by a large majority of the indentured laborers who arrived in Mauritius in the nineteenth century, and was soon adopted by immigrants from other backgrounds to become the de facto language of communication among Indo-Mauritians (even some Creoles and Sino- and Franco-Mauritians learned Bhojpuri for ease of communication).

Although its use is fast declining in favor of Kreol, many older members of the Indo-Mauritian community (including Hindus, Tamils, Muslims, and

Christians) still speak Bhojpuri in rural areas in the north. It is the mother tongue of around 15 percent of the population. The language can also be heard on television and radio, in films, talk shows, and music that is popular among many Mauritians.

Mauritian Bhojpuri has adapted to its new environment, and consequently many Kreol, French, and English words have given it a distinctly Mauritian feel. Unlike the situation in India, it is largely a spoken language and its users are unlikely to be proficient in its written form in the Devanagari script. The Mauritius Bhojpuri Institute and the Department of Bhojpuri, Folklore, and Oral Traditions at the island's Mahatma Gandhi Institute were established in 1982 in order to promote the use of the language. There have also been more recent, unsuccessful efforts to promote Bhojpuri among the younger generation of Indo-Mauritians, who are sometimes reluctant to learn a language they perceive as a backward, rural dialect.

Other Languages

To state that French, English, Kreol, and Bhojpuri are the only languages used in modern Mauritius would be a gross oversimplification. The reality is that many other languages are used as a way of marking one's proximity to one's presumed ancestors or religious community. Thus, Tamil, Telugu, Marathi, and Gujarati are claimed to be the ancestral languages of many Indo-Mauritians. Urdu is claimed by some Muslims (although many Mauritian Muslims have traditionally spoken Bhojpuri and Kreol), and Hakka, Cantonese, and sometimes Mandarin are the recognized languages of the small Sino-Mauritian community. One issue you will encounter is that it is often difficult to know whether people actually use these languages or if they are merely claiming to speak them as part of identity politics on the island. Furthermore, languages that may not necessarily be the mother tongue of any Mauritians have often been used as a sign of religious attachment, with Hindi, Arabic, and Latin being used among Hindus, Muslims, and Franco-Mauritian Catholics respectively.

CONVERSATION AND CHOOSING THE RIGHT LANGUAGE

One of the issues surrounding the multilingual nature of Mauritian public life is choosing which language to use when meeting someone outside your immediate circle of friends and relatives. The fact that practices vary from person to person only adds to the confusion. As a general rule, it would be normal to speak French to someone you are meeting for the first time, especially in settings where a certain degree of respect is expected (for example, in a business meeting). For close friends and relatives it would be more natural to speak to each other in Kreol. Kreol is also more commonly used in working-class life, especially among unskilled workers such as cleaners and laborers.

There are exceptions, however: Franco-Mauritians often use French in all contexts, both in public and at home; Mauritian parents might speak to their young children in French (supposedly to give them a head start when learning French at school), but will switch to Kreol when they are older; and a small number of families will speak South Asian languages (Bhojpuri, say) at home, but will use Kreol and French in daily life.

Although most Mauritians will be happy to speak to foreigners in French or English, some knowledge of Kreol will go a long way when you meet locals. If you are listening to Kreol, you will probably notice that expressions are peppered with images from Mauritian food and the natural environment. For instance, a Mauritian might say "*Karo kan finn pren difé*," meaning quite literally, "The sugarcane field has caught fire." What this really means is that someone has had a drastic haircut—or, more colloquially in English, that they have been attacked with a lawnmower.

Titles and Forms of Address

French practice predominates in this area, especially when meeting strangers. Therefore, *Monsieur* (*Misié* in Kreol, Sir or Mr. in English), *Madame* (*Madam* in Kreol, Madam or Mrs. in English), and *Mademoiselle* (*Mamzel* in Kreol, Miss in English) are used in general as a sign of respect. As in French culture, particular care should be taken to use a polite, respectful form of address when speaking to strangers and elders. Thus, the French *vous* (*ou* in Kreol) should be used formally, whereas the more informal *tu* (*to* or *twa* in Kreol) is acceptable among friends, relatives, and close colleagues, and also when speaking to children. Elders are sometimes called *tonton* (or *ton*) or *tantine* (uncle or auntie) as a traditional sign of respect, irrespective of whether or not you share blood ancestry. You might also hear people calling each other (and you) *cousin* or *cousine*, also regardless of family ties. This is often a way for peers to try to be familiar with you or even get close to you in order to do business.

In the Indo-Mauritian community specific names are given to relatives as part of an elaborate system differentiating between relatives on the paternal and maternal sides; these names are also widely known to members of other communities. *Chacha* is one's paternal uncle (also the nickname of Sir Seewoosagur Ramgoolam), *poupou* one's paternal aunt, *dada* one's paternal grandfather, and *dadi* one's paternal grandmother. On the mother's side, *mamou* refers to an uncle, *mami* to an aunt, *nana* to a grandfather, and *nani* to a grandmother.

Rural Mauritians may be reluctant to address you by your first name, even if you suggest it. Romantic partners use a number of terms of endearment—you will probably hear the most commonly used one, *gaté* (sweetheart).

Swearwords
Mauritian swearwords, like English ones, tend to focus on the physical side of life and the sexual organs. Many are sexist, misogynistic displays of masculinity, and greater insult is added if one insults another's mother or sister. You are likely to hear a number of such unsavory outbursts in daily life, and homophobic insults abound. Many Mauritians also draw imagery from everyday life to create ribald, earthy insults.

Foreigners should think twice before using swearwords. It could cause great offense in the company of women, children, or the older generation. Among macho men, however, it could gain you kudos—or, alternatively, physical injury.

HUMOR

Mauritians enjoy joking and teasing in everyday life. People may poke fun at the supposed ignorance and backwardness of rural life, or at corruption, nepotism, and the Mauritian propensity to be late. The taboo surrounding adultery is dealt with in jokes, but rarely in the company of women, children, or elders. Humorous cartoons and caricatures are common in the press, usually using Kreol in the dialogue. On television and in theaters, *Komiko* is a popular slapstick sketch show featuring Creoles in dysfunctional families.

A LANGUAGE OF NUMBERS

A peculiarity of Kreol is the strange use of specific numbers to refer to people and objects. This form of numerical slang includes:

4 (*quatre*)—death
5 (*cinq*)—Muslim
6 (*six*)—a homosexual man
9 (*neuf*)—never
22 (*vingt-deux*)—Hindu or shoes
27 (*vingt-sept*)—policeman
32 (*trente-deux*)—Chinese
35 (*trente-cinq*)—girlfriend or attractive woman

GREETINGS

Mauritians tend to be very polite to friends and strangers alike. It is quite normal to greet strangers on the street, although Westernization and growing individualism are fast eroding this practice among younger people. Greetings in Mauritius are a combination of Creole, French, British, and South Asian traditions, and will vary according to the identities of the people holding the conversation. Many young people are increasingly influenced by French expressions and pronunciation, but older, more conservative members of particular communities often use specific phrases among themselves—Hindi greetings such as *namasté* (with a slight bow and the palms of one's hands brought together) and Muslim greetings such as *salam alaykum*, for example. Out of politeness, it is common practice to inquire after a person's relatives or even to ask someone to pass on your regards (*konpliman* in Kreol).

SOME KREOL GREETINGS
Bonzour (*Bonjour*) Hello/good morning
Bonswar (*Bonsoir*) Good evening
Ki manyer? or *Sa va?* How are you? (the reply is *Korek*, meaning "Fine," *Byen*, "Well," or *Kom-si, kom-sa*, "So-so")
Ki pozision? How are things?
Ki nouvel? What's your news?/How are things?
Mersi Thank you
Orevwar (*Au revoir*), *Bye*, or
Ciao, or *Salam* among older Mauritians (not just Muslims) Good-bye

BODY LANGUAGE

Mauritians are relatively reserved in terms of physical contact with others. Although certain practices such as handshaking and *la bise* (French-style kissing on the cheek) are widespread, a substantial distance is maintained between people outside one's immediate family and close friends (around two feet is quite normal).

Many Mauritian men, especially members of traditional Muslim families, are unaccustomed to shaking hands with women, so situations where this might occur could cause some embarrassment. It would be safer to smile politely and nod when meeting a member of the opposite sex, but this could differ if the setting were very informal—meeting a Mauritian partner's close family or friends, for example, which could involve handshaking or even kissing.

If someone offers to kiss you (normally once on each cheek), you can take this as meaning you have been accepted as a trusted friend. Kissing is common among women, and between men and women, and adults and children, but is normally avoided between men, unless the people meeting are considered family or close friends. It is quite normal for friends and relatives to touch each other on the shoulder or pat each other on the back, but touching strangers would cause some unease.

Despite this physical distance between people, hand gestures and body language are used to great effect by Mauritians. Waving one's arms around to stress a point is not uncommon, and wild physical exaggeration is something you will get used to. Surprise, pain, or annoyance is often accompanied by the exclamation "*ayo!*", which you will hear on a daily basis. Many other gestures follow body language that is typically French.

THE MEDIA
The Press

One of the first newspapers to be published in the Africa region was *Le Cernéen*, a Mauritian publication with interests in the sugar industry, printed between 1832 and 1982. Its founder, Adrien d'Épinay, campaigned against censorship of the press, which would have an impact on Mauritian print journalism in the years to come.

For a small island with a relatively small population, modern Mauritius has a large number of newspapers and magazines. Freedom of the press is enshrined in the Constitution, and the dozens of newspapers and magazines often publish articles critical of the government and the different political parties, generating a healthy debate. There have been only a handful of cases where journalists have been imprisoned for their comments.

Mauritians like to read about scandals and corruption, celebrities vacationing on the island, local crimes and murders, sports, and arts and entertainment. The most widely read papers are the daily *L'Express* and *Le Mauricien*, and the weekly *Week-End*; others include *Le Matinal* and *Le Militant*. The majority are written in French, with the exception of token articles in English, and the

English-language weekly *Mauritius Times*, and others written in Indian and Chinese languages.

Television and Radio

The Mauritius Broadcasting Corporation, the state-run broadcasting service, provides television and radio coverage to the nation, including Rodrigues and Agalega. MBC derives its revenue from license fees and advertising, and is governed by state employees. It broadcasts news, sports, education, culture, and entertainment programs in a number of local languages, including French, English, Kreol, Bhojpuri, Hindi, and other South and East Asian (Chinese) languages. However, in general French is promoted to the detriment of other languages, and many foreign series are dubbed in French.

Three analog television channels are accessible to a majority of the population (MBC1, MBC2, and MBC3). Digital television is expanding quickly, and several channels offer a wide selection of films, sports, news, and entertainment. Channels in French, English, and Hindi—including Canal France Internationale and Réseau France Outre-Mer, BBC and Sky News, and Indian channel Doordarshan, respectively—allow the population to keep in touch with developments in countries with a huge cultural influence on Mauritius.

Five MBC radio stations offer music, news, culture, and education: RM1, RM2, Kool FM, Taal FM, and World Hit Radio. Other private radio stations such as Radio One, Radio Plus, and Radio Moris have been permitted since 2002, often with a focus on news, sports, popular music, and sometimes repetitive rounds of sega.

SERVICES
Mail

Mauritius Post is the reliable state postal service. It has existed in various guises since 1772 (La Poste in French, Lapos in Kreol), and also provides Internet, telephone facilities, and financial services.

Mauritian stamps often show iconic representations of the island's culture, history, and natural environment. In fact, Mauritius is a godsend for philatelists, who can visit the Postal Museum and the Blue Penny Museum in Port Louis, where very rare and beautiful stamps are on display (the nineteenth-century red penny and blue two-penny stamps are world-renowned).

Stamps can be bought in the many post offices across the island, and also at local shops. Since mailboxes do not exist, to mail a letter you must visit a post office or designated shop. Chargeable *poste restante* (general delivery) facilities are available at the General Post Office in Port Louis, and national and international courier and shipping services also operate from the island.

Telephone

Mauritius Telecom provides an efficient landline telephone network across the island. Many families have landlines, but coin- and credit card-operated public phones are also widely available. It is often cheaper to use calling cards for international calls.

Cell phone services are reliable, and network coverage is available across almost all of mainland Mauritius. A majority of the adult population uses relatively cheap cell phone technology. Emtel and state-owned CellPlus (a subsidiary of Mauritius

Telecom) are two of the main providers; both provide international roaming.

Telephone directories are widely available in homes, businesses, and hotels. The national operator can be reached on 150. The international dialing code for Mauritius is 230, which is followed by the seven-digit local number in full.

Internet

Mauritius has been moving steadily toward widespread Internet use. With the second-highest proportion of households with a computer in the Africa region, 19 percent of the population has access to the Internet at home and many more use it in Internet cafés in towns and tourist areas across the island. High-speed broadband has yet to be rolled out across the country, however, and Internet use has not spread widely beyond the wealthy middle-classes. Providers include Mauritius Telecom, Emtel, Nomad, and Telecom Plus.

CONCLUSION

Mauritius is a paradox. Some commentators invoke the idea of a "rainbow," or a multicultural haven of peace and understanding. Others, such as Malcolm de Chazal, see it as an ethnically divided island cultivating only "sugarcane and prejudice." Opinions differ as to whether it is a Creole island, a Hindu-dominated Little India, or a neocolonial outpost of the French-speaking world. Optimists see it as the biggest social and economic miracle of the postcolonial world, whereas pessimists believe it to be a social accident waiting to happen.

Mauritius has changed dramatically in recent years. It may be small and remote, but today it is ideally placed to compete in a globalized world. Its plural and democratic political system has been instrumental in accommodating the viewpoints of disparate ethno-religious communities, and its openness to foreigners has driven its economic success. Although daily life is far from idyllic for the majority of people struggling to reconcile their traditional culture with the demands of the modern world, many enjoy a comfortable lifestyle that would amaze their not-so-distant forebears who arrived from all corners of the globe.

The question of "Mauritianness" preoccupies the islanders. There is also an element of defensive pride in distinguishing themselves as neither African nor Asian. Nevertheless, there is still a tendency to break off into factions and divide along conservative ethno-religious lines. While communal relations are far from perfect, however, Mauritius provides a fascinating example of different people trying to live together in the best way that they can. If you show interest, courtesy and respect, you will be warmly received by many patient, friendly people who are keen to welcome outsiders. A local joke says quite aptly that "Mauritians are the tomato of the Indian Ocean—we go with everything."

Further Reading

In English

Ammigan, T. *Tamils in Mauritius*. Port Louis, Mauritius: Proag Printing, 1989.

Bernardin de Saint-Pierre, Jacques-Henri. *Journey To Mauritius*. Translated by Jason Wilson. Oxford: Signal [1773], 2002.

———. *Paul and Virginia*. Translated by John Donovan. London: Peter Owen [1787], 2005.

Boswell, Rosabelle. *Le Malaise Créole: Ethnic Identity in Mauritius*. New York and Oxford: Berghahn Books, 2006.

Carpooran, Arnaud. *Diksioner Morisien* (Mauritian Kreol Dictionary). Sainte-Croix, Mauritius: Koleksion Text Kreol Ltée, 2009.

Durrell, Gerald. *Golden Bats and Pink Pigeons*. Chichester: Summersdale, 2007.

Eisenlohr, Patrick. *Little India: Diaspora, Time, and Ethnolinguistic Belonging in Hindu Mauritius*. Berkeley, Los Angeles, and London: University of California Press, 2006.

Eriksen, Thomas Hylland. *Common Denominators: Ethnicity, Nation-Building and Compromise in Mauritius*. Oxford and New York: Berg, 1998.

Félix, Guy. *Genuine Cuisine of Mauritius*. Rose-Hill, Mauritius: Éditions de l'Océan Indien [1988], 2008.

Kanitkar, V. P., and W. Owen Cole. *Hinduism: An Introduction*. London: Hodder, 2010 (3rd edition).

Le Comte, Christian (ed.). *Travellers: Classic Journals and Accounts of Travellers to Mauritius*. Grand Baie, Mauritius: Mauritiana, 2008.

Lee, Jacques K. *Mauritius: Its Creole Language. The Ultimate Phrase Book and Dictionary*. London: Nautilus, 2003 (2nd edition).

———. *Sega: The Mauritian Folk Dance*. London: Nautilus, 1990.

O'Brian, Patrick. *The Mauritius Command*. London: Harper Perennial [1977], 2010

Pinto-Correia, Clara. *Return of the Crazy Bird: The Sad, Strange Tale of the Dodo*. New York: Springer-Verlag, 2003.

Vaughan, Megan. *Creating The Creole Island: Slavery in Eighteenth-Century Mauritius*. Durham, NC and London: Duke University Press, 2005.

Vine, David. *Island of Shame: The Secret History of the U.S. Military Base on Diego Garcia*. Princeton, NJ: Princeton University Press, 2009.

In French

Le Clézio, Jean-Marie Gustave and Jémia. *Sirandanes*. Paris: Seghers [1990], 2005.

Pyamootoo, Barlen. *Bénarès*. Paris: Éditions de l'Olivier/Le Seuil, 1999.

Wiltz, Marc and Pierre Astier (eds.). *Nouvelles de l'île Maurice*. Paris: Magellan, 2007.

Index

Acknowledgments

I would like to thank Marie-Anne Hintze, Roshni Mooneeram, and other staff at the University of Leeds for first introducing me to the Kreol language of Mauritius. I am also grateful to staff at the School of Oriental and African Studies (University of London) and Stanfords map and travel bookshop in London. Ravi Sahai and Paul Wilmot deserve my gratitude for their information and advice, and I thank the Rose, Pompon, Umrit, and Gujadhur families for their warmth and generosity in Mauritius and around the world. Finally, I must acknowledge my parents and family, who first encouraged my interest in foreign languages and cultures.